PRISCILLA HAUSER'S FOLK ART PAINTING FOR HOME DECORATION

Priscilla Hauser

Prentice Hall Press • New York

Published by Prentice Hall Press
A Division of Simon & Schuster, Inc.
Gulf + Western Building
One Gulf + Western Plaza
New York, NY   10023

PRENTICE HALL PRESS is a trademark of Simon & Schuster, Inc.

Library of Congress Cataloging-in-Publication Data
Hauser, Priscilla.
Priscilla Hauser's folk art painting for home
decoration.

Includes index.
1. Tole painting.   2. Painting—Technique.   3. Folk
art.   I. Title.   II. Title: Folk art painting for
home decoration.
TT385.H36   1986   745.7′2   86-12232
ISBN 0-13-710823-0

Manufactured in the United States of America

10   9   8   7   6   5   4   3   2

First Edition

Acknowledgments

Many thanks to Naomi Meeks, Sue Sensintaffar, Evelyn Carter, Peggy Crow, David and Carol Mays, A.J. Bartholomew, Juli Allen, Virginia Lou Greer, Tella Huntley, Linda Rudisill, Arthur Wynne, Robert Simmons, Dennis Kapp, and Jim Harkness for all your valuable help.

Contents

Introduction—Transformagic!

There they are, the most wonderful things in the world—the things found in the attic, in the basement, at flea markets. In the world of tole and decorative painting, the old can be magically transformed into lovely home accessories. I like to call it *Transformagic*. Indeed it is magic, but it is magic that can be learned by absolutely everyone. It is exciting and so much fun!

It takes time to learn to paint; it takes practice, too, but it's rewarding in so many ways. You can paint things for your home, gifts for others, or, if you desire, you can paint and sell your work. Yes you can! People often think that they would never be good enough. That is not true at all. Even after all these years, there are still times when I paint something that doesn't turn out right. When that happens, I sign someone else's name to it and sell it! Not really of course, but . . . . On the other hand, you're probably a lot better than you think you are, and there is a market for your work. If you can stand to part with it

Priscilla Hauser at work.

once you have completed it, you might very well be able to sell it.

For many, the "first" learning experience is somewhat demanding. I promise you, though, that if you will stick to it, you will find that the pleasure painting brings is incredible. You will want to paint more than you will want to cook, sew, or perhaps even eat.

Some of my favorite things (besides my husband, Jerry, and the children) consist of both old and new camelback trunks, little school desks, old table leaves, music boxes, eggs of all sizes and shapes, baskets, ribbons, and lace. All of these things can be transformed into "heirlooms" through painting.

In this book, I have provided folk art designs and instructions that will enable you to do decorative painting on all sorts of objects.

If you want to paint, join hands with me. Through the pages of this book, you will learn not only to paint, but to see things in a new and different way.

With brush in hand, my mind empties of its sorrows and the beauty of the simple things around me takes on new meaning—the beauty in life smiles!

So get busy, go to the art store or the craft store. Purchase the paint, the materials, and supplies. Dig out all those old treasures. Make the decision to spend an hour or two a day doing nothing but practicing. If you do this every day for two months, you will have learned how to paint these designs. Remember that the decorative painting you learn to do today will be tomorrow's folk art. I can teach anyone to do decorative painting, and I love doing it. Believe me, I can teach you, too.

1 The Fundamentals

Terminology

PLEASE read this chapter before you try to paint. If you don't understand the terminology I'm using, you will not fully appreciate what I am trying to say.

Paint Consistency

Paint consistency is one of the most important factors in painting. Yet in all the years I have been teaching people to paint, proper consistency is the thing that I have the hardest time getting them to understand. Paint consistency is just like the temperature setting in your oven. You can't bake with the oven set at the same temperature for everything you are going to bake. Likewise, when you paint, you need different consistencies for the different things you are painting.

Oil paint comes from the tube in different consistencies, depending upon the pigments that were used to make the particular color. The amount of turp you need to add to the paint depends upon the color and the amount of paint you have squeezed on your palette. Rarely would you use paint as it comes directly from the tube to the palette. Instead, take a palette knife and whip the paint to mix it with any oil that might have separated from the pigment.

To achieve the proper consistency for what you are going to paint, add odorless turp to the paint, mixing it firmly with the palette knife, until the correct consistency is achieved. This takes some time and work.

When you do brush-stroke work (defined in chapter 2), the paint must have a very, very thin (almost what I jokingly call a "bird blessing") consistency. In other words, loose; a lot of turp must be added to the pigment. When you pick the pigment up on your palette knife, it should fall loosely from your palette knife and go "splat" on the palette. When you are dry-brush blending (defined in chapter 2), the paint must have a thicker consistency—that of spreadable butter or mayonnaise. When

you blend, the paint must not be too thin, or overblending and muddying can easily occur.

There are other consistencies that will be described throughout this book. Pay attention to the proper paint consistency; it has a *major* effect on your finished painting.

Colorbook Painting

Colorbook painting is filling in between the lines with a solid color, just as if you were coloring in a coloring book.

Undercoating

I do not like beginners to undercoat. I like them to learn to blend using a very light touch, so that their painting technique will really develop. As a matter of fact, I even recommend that beginners paint on a black background. That way, if the beginner presses too hard when blending, the black color will show through. This exercise forces you to learn to blend using a light touch. However, when you are painting on very dark backgrounds, it is wonderful to be able to undercoat with white or other colors; the light undercoat makes the finished painting much brighter.

If you choose to undercoat, it must be done in a very smooth, neat way. Otherwise, the undercoat will show through your painting and be more of a hindrance than a help.

When I undercoat, I use an old red-sable brush that has been washed thoroughly in soap and water to remove all oil residue. I use my white acrylic basecoat, for it is very smooth and creamy. I then apply a very thin coat of acrylic to the design. I let it dry thoroughly and then apply another thin coat, and even a third coat if necessary.

If you are going to undercoat, I must stress that it is vital to undercoat precisely within the lines of the design, very neatly and very smoothly, or you will have problems.

Outlining

Outlining is generally done with a #1 red-sable liner brush or the fine point of any good brush. When you outline, you want to get your liner brush completely full of very thin paint—the consistency of ink. Twist the brush to a point, then outline using a very light touch.

Double Loading

Double loading means carrying two colors side by side on the brush. I will try very hard to teach you how to double load properly later on in this book. It is a very important technique.

Basic Brush Strokes

Basic brush strokes are really like the letters of the alphabet, though there are fewer brush strokes than there are letters, and it will be easier to learn the brush strokes than it was for you to learn to form the letters of the alphabet. Basic brush strokes are very important to good painting technique; please learn them well. Basic brush strokes are done with the round and flat brushes as well as with the liner brush.

Dry-brush Blending

Dry-brush blending is the second technique needed to learn to paint. Dry-brush blending means blending or shading two or more colors together. When you dry-brush blend, your paint must have a much thicker consistency than it does for brush-stroke work.

Cross Blending

Cross blending means pulling the dark shading color across to the light or the light shading color across to the dark. Cross blending is often needed to move a color from one side of an object to another. We rarely leave an item in a cross-blended state; we go back and blend it lightly, following the natural direction of the object that we are painting.

Overblending

Overblending occurs when you work the paint to death. It causes "muddiness," and it happens when you use too much pressure on the brush, when the paint is too thin, or when you simply blend too long. One of the most difficult parts of learning to blend is learning when to stop. This comes with practice. When the subject you are blending looks good to you, then STOP. You must also learn to blend using a "light touch."

Dirty Brush

A dirty brush is a brush that has paint in it; it has been wiped on a soft, absorbent rag—not cleaned in turp but simply wiped. I will often tell you to "double load a dirty brush." This means that if you don't have a brush that is already dirty, pick one up, fill it with paint, wipe it on an absorbent rag, and then double load (see pages 11–12), using the dirty brush for one side and the suggested color on the other side. Most of the time, we want to dry-brush blend using a dirty brush or a brush that we have wiped. Otherwise, if we put a clean brush down on what we are blending, we will lift too much paint away.

Blend on Palette to Soften Color

Throughout this text I will tell you to double load your brush or to double load a dirty brush. Then I will say, "blend on palette to soften color." This means exactly what it says: just blend in *one spot* on your palette to soften or merge the two colors together before you go on and do your painting.

Contrast

Contrast is the key to beautiful painting. You have to learn to paint with contrast, not only within the subject you are painting, but between things. For example, when you are learning to paint leaves, leaves that are in the back of the design must be dark, those in the middle must be medium-value, and those in the front must be light. You must paint with contrast between the three sets of leaves. Any time that two edges come together, of course, the edge that is to the front is generally lighter, and the edge to the back is darker. This creates contrast. Contrast makes your painting look alive.

Oil Paint

There are several different types of paints; oils are my favorite. Oils consist of pigment that is ground in a vehicle—usually linseed oil. Oils are slow to dry, therefore giving you plenty of time to work them and create beauty. Many oil colors are very opaque, and I find this to be an advantage.

Acrylics

Acrylics are actually plastic—a polymer emulsion. They dry rapidly; their solvent is water. The acrylic colors are not nearly as opaque as oil colors. Acrylics are fun to work with, but I still find oils to be the "Grand Madame" of painting.

Controlled Consistency

Controlled consistency means exactly what it sounds like—*you* control the consistency of your paint. Let's say, for example, that the paint on your palette is the consistency of soft butter, but you need to double load your brush, which requires using a thinner consistency. Rather than having to mix another palette of paint very thin, you can control the consistency from thick to thin by touching the turp (touch the hairs of the red-sable brush to the turp), blotting on the rag, and thinning the paint in your brush.

Supplies

This section will tell you everything you need to know about the supplies you will need for your painting. Most of the supplies are readily available at art- and craft-supply stores, but check Sources for a list of mail-order suppliers.

Paints

My world of painting can be done with oils or acrylics. Oils are my favorites—they are truly a "class act." It is also fun to paint with acrylics, however, so you might want to paint the same design with oils and acrylics and make the decision yourself. I have used oils in this book, with the exception of backgrounds.

Oil paints come in the most fabulous array of colors imaginable, and it is great fun to go into an art or craft store and buy all the wonderful colors. I have provided a list of colors that I feel are essential to getting started. You can add other colors that are exciting to you as you develop your skills and techniques. I enjoy using Permalba Oil Colors, largely for the following reasons:

- The consistency of Permalba Oils is absolutely incredible—they are beautifully soft and creamy.
- The colors are gorgeous and exciting. There is a difference between the same color in different brands of paint. For example, Permalba Burnt Umber is a relatively light Burnt Umber.
- The opacity of the Permalba colors is unique. They contain a lot of pigment, so they cover beautifully.

However, in my paint box you will find several different brands. If a company manufactures a color I feel I simply cannot live without, I will certainly purchase it.

The following is a list of oil colors that I have used in this book. All oil paints are semitransparent because they consist of pigment ground in a vehicle of linseed oil, and it is the nature of linseed oil to be transparent. Nevertheless, oils are still divided into two categories: transparent and opaque. I have designated this by placing a "T" (for transparent) or "O" (for opaque) next to the names of the recommended colors.

Permalba White (O)
Ice Blue (O)
Burnt Umber (O)
Burnt Sienna (O)
Yellow Citron (O)
Cadmium Yellow Light (O)
Cadmium Yellow Medium (O)
Lamp Black (O)
Ivory Black (O)
Paynes Gray (O)
Burnt Alizarin (O)
Prussian Blue (T)
Ultramarine Blue (T)
Cadmium Orange (O)
Asphaltum (T)
Permalba Mauve (T)
Cadmium Red Light (O)
Cadmium Red Medium (O)

Leaf Green Light (O)
Leaf Green Medium (O)
Leaf Green Dark (O)

There is a set of Permalba Oils that contains 18 tubes of my favorite colors. This set can be found in art and craft stores throughout the United States and Canada.

Brushes

Please invest in good brushes. I know they cost a lot of money, but I would rather you have only two or three good brushes than half a dozen bad ones. In the techniques that I am teaching, using fine brushes is imperative if you are to execute the brush strokes and paint well.

I recommend red-sable brushes. (These brushes are actually made from the tail of the Kolinsky, a little animal that is a member of the weasel family.) The hair of the Kolinsky grows and develops best in the cold climate of Siberia. The hair is actually graded and sorted, and the brushes are made by hand.

You will need flat red-sable brushes in different sizes. When you are painting small designs, you need small brushes; medium-size brushes are used for medium-size designs, and, of course, large brushes are needed for large designs.

The flat red-sable brushes are beautiful tools, and they come in sizes 00 through 20. My favorite red-sable brushes are made in the United States to my specifications by the Robert Simmons Company, and they are fully guaranteed.

You will also need round red-sable brushes as well as a #1 liner (figure 1-1). I recommend #2, #8, and #12 Priscilla Hauser flat red-sable tole brushes; a #3 round red-sable watercolor brush; and a #1 liner or scroll brush (see Sources). Eventually, you will want to invest in a flat red-sable brush in at least every other size from a 00 through a 20.

Cleaning and Care of Brushes. It is extremely important to clean your brushes thoroughly. In my many years of traveling and teaching, I am always amazed to see that people never quite get all the oil paint out of the hair of the red-sable brush. They think they do, but they don't.

Before you begin to paint, you must "break in" a new brush. Just as a pair of shoes has to be broken in in order to be comfortable and to serve you well, so does a brush.

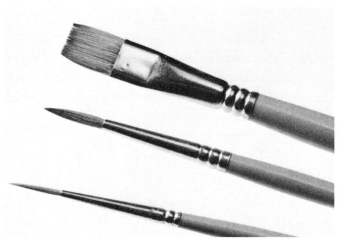

1-1. Flat and round red-sable brushes.

Most fine brushes come with sizing in them. Sizing is a stiffening agent that keeps every hair in place. It is important to work all of the sizing out of your brush and then to clean the brush in turp. Use turp and Brush Creme and work the Brush Creme thoroughly through the hairs of the brushes. Take your time. It takes two or three minutes to break a brush in properly.

After you have finished painting for the day, clean the brush in your odorless turp as thoroughly as you can. Place a little Brush Creme in the lid of the Brush Creme jar and, using the turp, continue to work the brush back and forth in the Brush Creme and turp. You will be amazed at the amount of paint that will come from the hairs of the brush.

Now shape the brush, leaving the Brush Creme in the brush. Store it with the handles down and the red-sable hairs up so that nothing will bend or bump into the hairs to misshape them in any way. When you are ready to paint again, simply rinse the brush in the odorless turp. The Brush Creme will rinse away and not hurt the turp, brush, or paint. Brush Creme keeps the brush in a wet state. It doesn't allow paint to dry in the brush and ruin it. What's more, it grooms and conditions your brush.

Other Types of Brushes. There are so many other types of brushes available that it can become very confusing.

Synthetic brushes are exactly what the name implies: they are made of synthetic fiber, not natural hair. Because synthetic brushes do not hold up as well as sable (the hairs will curl), I do not use them except when I absolutely have to. I might, for example, use a synthetic brush when I paint on an extremely rough surface, such as old barn wood, or when I scrub a background on canvas. Some people like to use synthetic brushes when they paint with acrylics, as water is hard on red sable.

In addition to synthetics, there are brushes made with a number of different types of animal hair. None of them is as fine as red sable, but they are better than synthetics.

A bristle brush is a very coarse brush often used in canvas painting and to create special effects.

I use many other types of brushes in my painting to achieve special effects, as well. For example, I use a fan-shaped brush for painting grass. I use a bristle scumbling brush (a stiff, round bristle brush) for adding texture to the center of a poppy. A Robert Simmons Silver Mop or Grape Blender is a special-effect brush used for gently brushing away brush strokes on a painting.

I could write a whole book just on the different types of hairs and fibers used in brush making and the special effects that brushes can create. You will learn about this as you paint and as you experience different brushes for yourself.

To begin, if you will do as I have suggested you will not go wrong.

Additional Materials

- A palette knife: My preference is a good straight-blade palette knife—one that is made of soft flexible steel, so that when I am mixing the paint and the turp, I can feel the consistency of my paint. A cheap palette knife is not made of good steel and will not enable you to feel that all-important paint consistency.
- A disposable tracing-paper palette pad: This pad serves two purposes. It is tracing paper on which you can trace and then transfer your designs, and it also serves as a wonderful matte palette for painting. A *matte surface* is excellent when learning to double load a brush because it is not too slick and will enable the brush to fill *properly*. Don't use wax-coated palettes when double loading.
- Odorless turp: Today there are wonderful turpentine substitutes available. They are not as strong as turpen-

tine, but they mix well with your oil paints and clean your brushes beautifully. I greatly appreciate a manufacturer's concern in producing low-odor oil colors and turp. My choice for a low-odor turp is a product that has been in existence for over 60 years, called Turpenoid.

- Soft absorbent rags or towels: Oh my goodness, is this ever important! An absorbent surface is essential for blotting your brushes, and the softness of the rag or towel you are blotting and wiping your brushes on is also extremely important. An inexpensive, rough towel will wear down the hairs of your brushes very fast. You can actually destroy a fine red-sable brush by wiping it on rough rags or toweling. Also, the soft absorbent rags must pull the proper amount of turp from the hairs of the red-sable brush when you dip it in the turp and blot it on the rag. The toweling that works best for me is Job Squad.
- Priscilla Hauser Brush Creme and conditioner: Brush Creme is wonderful, for it not only enables you to clean your brushes thoroughly, it also conditions them. *It is very important that your brushes are kept clean and in excellent condition!*
- White chalk: White chalk is used for chalking the back of the traced design and then transferring it to your prepared surface. Do not use the dustless kind.
- A wide-mouth container for turp: Of course, a wide-mouth jar will work, but there is a brush basin available from art and craft stores that is really terrific.

Transferring Patterns

Some of the designs in this book have been reduced in size to fit on the book page. The caption indicates by how much the design has been reduced. The easiest way to enlarge these patterns is to take them to a photostat shop and have them professionally enlarged to the size you want.

Use tracing paper and a fine-point marking pen or pencil to make a careful tracing of the pattern from the book. You may transfer the pattern with graphite paper or by chalking the back of the tracing. I prefer using chalk because the lines can always be removed after an item is painted. Graphite paper lines sometimes show and are almost impossible to remove.

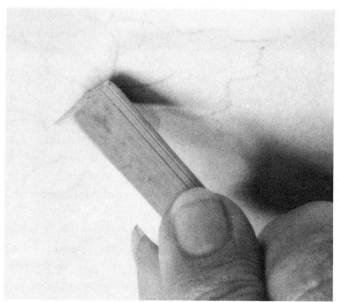

1-2. The chalk method—step 1.

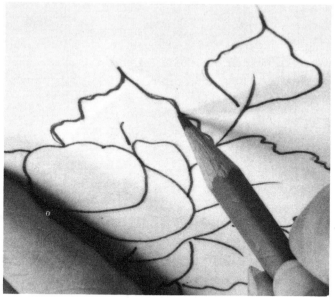

1-3. The chalk method—step 3.

Chalk Method

Let's talk about transferring with chalk first. If the item to be decorated is a medium to a dark color, use white chalk on the back of the tracing. If the background is white or a light color, use light green or light yellow chalk. Then do the following:

1. On the back side of the tracing, go over the lines of the pattern firmly with chalk. Never rub chalk all over the back of the pattern (figure 1-2).
2. Shake off the excess dust.
3. Center the pattern on the item to be painted; secure it carefully with masking tape if you wish (the tape could pull off the background color). Go over the pattern lines with a sharp-pointed pencil or stylus. Do not press hard with the pencil; you do *not* want to make an indentation on the surface below (figure 1-3).

Graphite Paper Method

To transfer with graphite paper, use white graphite on dark backgrounds and gray graphite on light backgrounds. If you are going to use a new piece of gray graphite, first wipe the graphite paper with a rag slightly dampened in turp to try and get as much of the graphite off as possible. This will help keep smudges to a minimum as you transfer the design to your prepared project. Then:

1. Position the pattern on the item to be decorated and secure it with masking tape if you wish.
2. Slip the carbon under the pattern, making sure the correct side is down, and transfer the pattern. Use light pressure on the pencil or stylus.

2 The Technique

Don't you dare skip over this chapter and go on to other things! *The basics are the most important part of learning to paint.* If you are going to build a house, you have to have a good foundation. If you want to paint, you need to develop a strong technique.

For starters we need to talk about the basics. The two partners in excellent painting—the foundation to all of painting, whether decorative painting, tole, or painting on canvas—are basic brush strokes and dry-brush blending.

Basic Brush Strokes

Basic brush strokes are painted with either flat or round brushes. In general, I use a flat brush more than a round brush, but, for strokes that are used in some of the European folk art, some flower petals, borders, and other strokes, the round red-sable watercolor brush is truly the right choice.

In order to paint beautiful brush strokes there are several points that must be carefully observed:

- You must have a fine brush that is in excellent condition! If you use a poor brush, I can promise that you will paint lousy brush strokes.
- For brush-stroke work, the paint must have a *very thin flowing consistency.* Please mix as much odorless turp into the paint as necessary. The paint should flow almost like ink flows from a pen.
- You must understand how brush strokes are constructed. A number of years ago I had an opportunity to teach in Japan. I taught two seminars in Tokyo and one in Kyoto. I was absolutely amazed at how beautifully the Japanese people did the brush strokes. All of a sudden I realized that their calligraphy consists of brush strokes; they have been doing these strokes as part of their handwriting technique all of their lives.

Flat Brush Strokes

Before you begin to paint these brush strokes, you must learn the parts of the flat brush. Figure 2-1 will show you what the parts are. The flat edge, or chisel edge, is very important. When you are painting on the flat edge of your brush, the handle of the brush is actually pointing straight up toward the ceiling.

There are two flat surfaces. The sides of the brush are called "chisel edges." The two corners of the brush are called "chisel corners."

For many years I have been writing books that feature my step-by-step paint-along worksheets. I sincerely hope you will read and reread the written instructions. (Keep this book in the bathroom, spend some time there, and read and study this book.) Then take the color worksheets and study them. Lay a sheet of transparent tracing paper on top of the worksheet, choose the appropriate brush size, and make your strokes right on top of mine many, many times. This is the next best thing to my being there with you to take your hand and guide you stroke by stroke

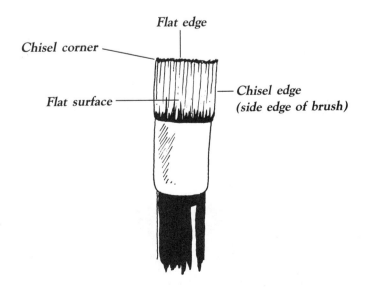

2-1. **Parts of the flat brush.**

8

through the painting of the leaves or any of the other subjects taught to you in this book.

Basic Stroke. The first stroke I call the basic stroke (figure 2-2). Be sure all the sizing or Brush Creme is out of your brush. Clean your brush in turp, blot it on your soft absorbent rag, and fill it completely on both sides with the very thin paint. Touch on the flat edge, press on the flat surface, hold the pressure, and pull. Look easy? It is easy.

Line Stroke. Fill the brush completely with paint, stand the brush on the flat edge with the handle pointing *straight up toward the ceiling*, and lightly drag on the flat edge of the brush to paint a line (figure 2-3).

Comma Stroke. The third and fourth strokes are comma strokes. We paint comma strokes that angle to the left and comma strokes that angle to the right. To paint a comma stroke that angles to the left, angle the flat edge of your brush toward the left corner of your practice sheet, as shown in figure 2-4. Touch on the flat edge, put pressure on the flat surface, and begin to pull; then lift back up on the flat edge and drag. *There is no twisting or turning of the brush.* Simply touch, press, pull, begin to lift, and drag.

Try making a little flag of masking tape and attaching it to the handle of the paint brush. When you are doing *most* of the brush strokes, the flag *should not wave*. It is simply a matter of touching, pressing, pulling, and lifting. If you try to turn the brush, the flag will wave; this means that you are not doing the strokes properly. The exception to this rule is when you paint half-circle strokes.

2-3. Line stroke.

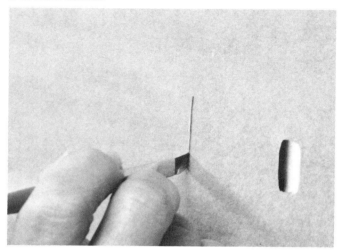

2-4. Comma stroke.

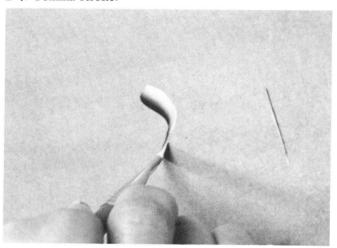

2-2. Basic stroke.

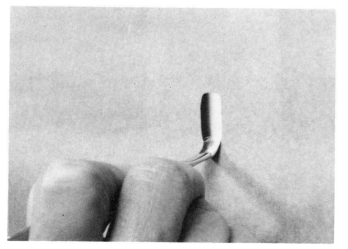

2-5. "S" stroke angled to the left.

2-6. "S" stroke angled to the right.

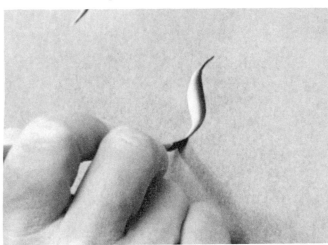

2-7. Rightside-up "U" stroke.

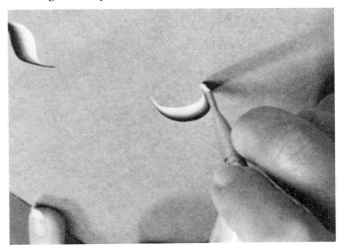

2-8. Half-circle stroke.

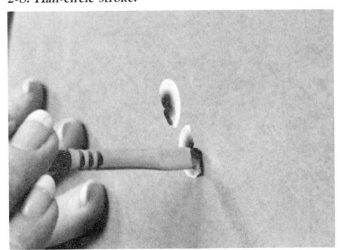

The comma stroke that angles to the right is the reverse of the stroke that angles to the left. Right-handed persons generally find it easier to make strokes that angle toward the left, whereas left-handed persons make strokes that angle toward the right more easily. However, both directions must be mastered.

"S" Stroke. The next strokes are called "S" strokes. They are very important. Fill the brush with thin, loose paint. Angle the flat edge of the brush toward the left corner, as shown in figure 2-5; stand the brush on the flat edge, slide applying gradual pressure, then gradually lift back up on the flat edge and drag.

Now, reverse the stroke and paint an "S" stroke angled to the right (figure 2-6).

Rightside-up "U" Stroke. Fill the brush full of thin, loose paint; stand the brush on the flat edge, slide down on the flat edge, gradually applying pressure, then lift back on the flat edge on the other side of the "U" (figure 2-7).

Upside-down "U" Stroke. This is the reverse of the rightside-up "U."

Half-Circle Stroke. We paint both rightside-up half circles and upside-down half circles (figure 2-8). To paint the half circle, fill the brush with thin, loose paint. Stand the brush on the flat edge, apply pressure, hold the pressure, and let the brush pivot in your fingers. Please note that this is the *first* time I have told you to twist or turn the brush in your fingers. All the other strokes have just been a matter of touching, pressing, lifting, and pulling.

There are many variations of all these strokes, but these are the basic flat brush strokes.

Round Brush Strokes

The round red-sable watercolor brush is a beautiful brush with which to execute the three brush strokes described below. There are variations of these brush strokes, but the three strokes I want you to learn are the polliwog, which is a straight stroke, and the two polliwog commas.

Polliwog. To paint the polliwog stroke, fill the brush completely with paint that is of a thin, loose consistency. Touch, apply pressure (the more pressure you apply the wider the hairs will spread apart), then begin to lift and drag, pulling toward the bottom of your practice page. Watch the hairs go back together. As you come to the

2-9. Polliwog.

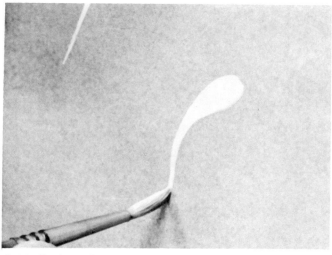

2-11. Right polliwog comma.

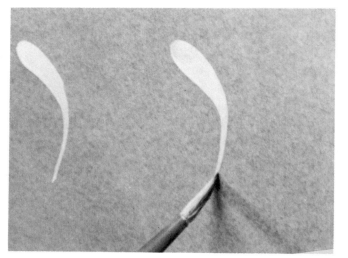

2-10. Left polliwog comma.

2-12. Strokes with the liner brush.

end of this stroke, you may have to twist or turn the brush slightly to the left or right to push the hairs together to form a point. You can paint big polliwogs, little polliwogs, short fat ones, or lean skinny ones (figure 2-9).

Commas. To paint a polliwog comma that angles to the left, fill the round brush with paint that has a very thin, loose consistency. Angle the brush toward the left corner of your practice sheet; touch, apply pressure, and begin to lift and drag, leaning to the inside edge of your brush, until a point is formed. No twisting or turning of the brush is necessary (figure 2-10).

For a polliwog comma that angles to the right, simply reverse this technique (figure 2-11).

Liner Brush Strokes

A #1 liner or scroll brush is a member of the round brush family. When you look at the brush you will see that the metal ferrel is round, just like the round watercolor brush. While this is the brush I do all my linework and curlicues with, it will also paint beautiful long, slender comma strokes, because it is a member of the round brush family.

Strokes are executed with the liner brush in the same way that they are with the round red-sable watercolor brush (figure 2-12). Remember that any time you do line-work or curlicues, the paint must be as thin as ink; the brush must be completely full of paint, and it must then be twisted to a point.

Double Loading

Double loading means carrying two or more colors on a red-sable brush at the same time. It is important that you learn to do this; don't let anyone tell you it is not. Painting is so much faster and easier once you actually have the technique of double loading under control.

If you want to paint a gorgeous rose, if you want to shade fruit and flowers properly, correct double loading of a brush is essential. Yes, it takes practice, darn it, to learn to do anything well. You have to practice and you have to "pay your dues." I promise it is worth it!

When you double load a brush, your paints have to be of the right consistency. Stop and think for a minute. If you are trying to fill a brush with paint that is too thick:

1. You won't get any paint in the brush.
2. You will never get any paint to flow from the brush.
3. You won't be able to double load the brush.

Paint consistency is the most important key to proper double loading. Paying attention to what you are actually doing on the palette is the next most important thing.

Discipline yourself to practice double loading for fifteen or twenty minutes each day for a few weeks and you will catch on to what you are doing. Let's practice with two inexpensive colors. Use Leaf Green Medium and Burnt Umber:

    1. Thin two quarter-size puddles of paint to the consistency of "bird blessings"—very, very loose.

    2. With your palette knife, push those puddles up so that they have a clean edge, as shown in figure 2-13.

    3. Now, with a #6 or #8 flat red-sable brush, clean your brush in turp and blot it on a soft, absorbent rag. Then "sneak up" to the edge of the lightest color first. Fill one edge of the brush with the light color, as shown in figure 2-14.

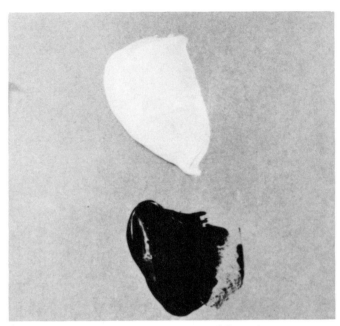

2-13. Start with two quarter-size puddles of paint.

2-14. Practice with a #6 or #8 flat red-sable brush.

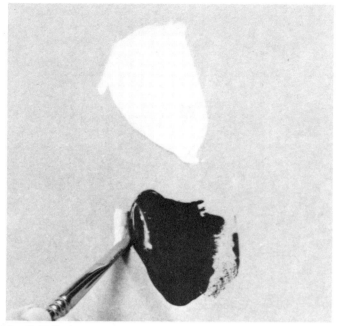

2-15. Fill the outer edge.

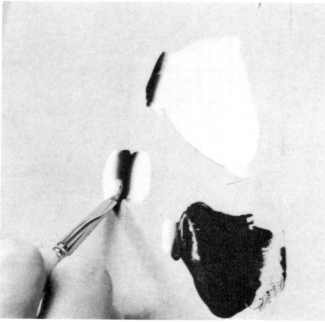

2-16. Blending.

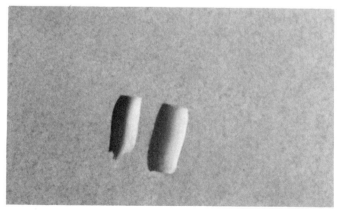

2-17. Colors blending in the center.

4. Fill the other edge with the Burnt Umber, as shown in figure 2-15.

5. Blend, blend, blend on your palette, as shown in figure 2-16. What you are actually doing is pushing the paint right through the hairs of the brush from front to back so that every single hair is saturated with paint. Now, turn the brush over and blend on the other side. At this point, you have just started to get that brush full of paint. You must not have a space between the green and umber in the center of the brush. The colors should gradually blend into each other in the center of the brush where they meet (figure 2-17).

6. Carefully go back and pick up more green.

7. Carefully go back and pick up more umber.

8. Go back to the same spot you blended and blend again. This way, you won't be "spending" the paint out of the brush all over the palette but blending in the same spot on the palette. You may have to go back four or five times to pick up enough paint to saturate the brush.

On the color worksheet (see W-2), look at the beautiful double-loaded brush strokes. Again, you will not do well unless you are:

1. Neat on your palette, paying attention to the edges.
2. Using paint of the proper consistency—very thin.
3. Using a brush that is completely full of paint. You must blend on both sides of the brush in order to push the paint completely through the hairs of the brush from front to back so that every single hair is saturated with paint.

Please don't be discouraged. It probably won't work for you the first few times you try—you will mess up your brush. When this happens, simply clean the brush and try again and again until you get it. You *will* get it if you try. Of course there are bound to be some moments of discouragement, but hang in there, baby, for learn you will, and I promise that the joys you will reap will be worth every bit of that learning experience.

Blending

The second partner is dry-brush blending. Dry-brush blending is exactly what it sounds like—blending or shading two or more colors together with a relatively dry brush. Do not use a brush that has been dipped in turp; this would cause your colors to run together. Your paint must be thicker in consistency when you do dry-brush blending so that overblending or "muddying" will not take place.

There are actually two types of dry-brush blending. One is done by stroking the paint; the other is done by actually patting the paint. Almost all dry-brush blending is done with a flat red-sable brush.

In order to learn to blend properly, you must develop a light touch. Many years ago, when I first began painting, I had a natural tendency to be very heavy-handed. I wanted to mash down on the paint to kill the colors. This simply doesn't get the job done. I developed a little exercise for blending two colors together. First, draw a long slender rectangle (figure 2-18). Put some Cadmium Yellow Medium and Prussian Blue on your palette. If necessary, add just a few drops of turp, for the paint must have the consistency of soft spreadable butter or cake icing. Paint 98 percent of the rectangle with Cadmium Yellow Medium. The remaining 2 percent should be filled in with Prussian Blue. Now, wipe your brush on a soft, absorbent rag. *Don't* put it in turp. Begin blending the Prussian Blue into the Yellow. Wipe, blend, wipe, blend; the idea is to blend from dark blue into dark green, getting lighter and lighter in green until you eventually end up in yellow. Never put the brush in turp. You can move the blue into the yellow and the yellow back up toward the blue. Don't be heavy-handed. If you are, you can mess up the entire exercise. When I am doing this exercise, I lay my left arm down and my right arm on top of it. When I start to get too heavy-handed with my right hand, I can actually feel the physical pressure of the right hand pressing down on the left, so I lighten my touch.

When stroke blending round objects, you can stroke from the top of the object to the bottom or from the bottom to the top. Always stroke blend following the natural curve of the object you are blending. On the right

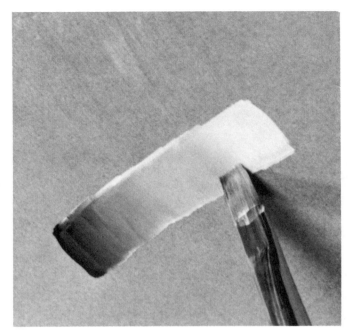

2-18. Developing a light touch.

2-19. Stroke blending a round object.

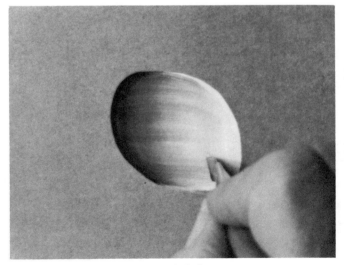

2-20. Pull the brush across lightly.

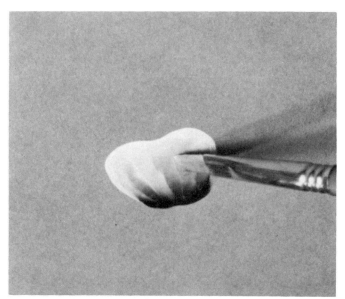

2-21. Patting and pulling motion.

side, curve to the right; on the left side, curve to the left, and in the middle, pull straight. Wipe the brush often, but not too often, for it is possible to wipe off all the paint onto the rag. Learning when to stop simply takes practice.

In figure 2-19, I have shown you how to stroke blend a round object. After you have stroke blended from the top to the bottom and the bottom to the top, it may be necessary to do something called *cross blending*. Sometimes when you are blending, the dark color will stay on one side and the light on the other side; you must therefore cross blend the object to get the colors to move from one side to the other. When you cross blend, pull across lightly, wiping the brush each time you cross blend (figure 2-20). You may cross blend from dark to light or light to dark. You almost never leave an object in a cross-blended

stage, for it would appear to be spinning. After the cross blending has been completed, wipe the brush and go back over the object lightly, following the natural direction of the object so that proper blending is completed.

Pat Blending

If you were to watch me pat blend two or more colors together, it would almost look like I was patting in an up-and-down motion or stippling the paint. This is not the way it is done at all. It is actually a "touch-pull, touch-pull" motion, done with very light strokes and using as large a brush as possible.

The example in figure 2-21 is that of a flower petal. It could be any type of a pat-blended flower petal.

First of all, you may want to stroke blend the dark color out into the light and/or the light color back down toward the dark.

Wipe and groom the brush. To groom a brush, I hold a tissue or soft rag in my hand and wipe the brush by gently pinching the hairs between the rag or tissue. This keeps every hair of the brush in place while you are pat blending.

With the patting and pulling motion, as you can see by studying figure 2-21, you are actually moving the dark color up over the light and the light color back down over the dark. Instead of doing it by stroking, however, you are doing it by patting, and a much softer look is achieved. This is the way we make flower petals ripple; it is the way we put folds in clothing. It is a more advanced form of blending. I will not be going into it in detail in this book, but I wanted you to see it and recognize it to understand what it is. When you pat blend, always follow the natural shape of the object you are blending.

3 Preparation of Surfaces

Proper preparation of the surfaces on which you are going to paint is extremely important. It is a shame to spend the time it takes to learn to paint and then have the surface on which you have painted peel or not hold up well simply because it was not properly prepared in the first place.

There can actually be so much involved in surface preparation that I could write a book on furniture finishing and refinishing alone. I will merely summarize in this chapter, trying to make preparation as quick and easy as possible, but still professional.

Old Wood

Let's talk about old wood first. When you are dealing with old pieces, there is often a finish that needs to be removed or at least stabilized before a new finish is applied.

If you have a wonderful old painted chair or wooden trunk, check to see how badly the paint is peeling. If it is peeling badly all over, the best thing to do is to strip it. Furniture stripping companies can usually be found in the yellow pages of the telephone directory. This is by far the easiest, and in many cases the least expensive, way. Paint removers are often harsh, strong products, and I do not like to breathe the fumes. Therefore, when I have pieces that require the removal of paint, I will have a professional strip them for me. There are various brands of paint removers available if you choose to do it yourself, but please read and follow the directions carefully.

After the paint has been removed, it may be a good idea to seal the wood with a good wood sealer, if it is porous and in bad shape. Sand, then apply the new paint.

If you are going to stain the wood, you will want to do the staining before a sealer is applied. Stain first, then seal, then sand.

New Wood

New wood may or may not require an initial sanding. Generally, I do not sand first unless it is absolutely necessary. Then, you will have to decide whether you are going to stain the wood or paint it.

If staining is your choice, the staining should be done first, then the sealing. If painting is your choice, paint first then seal.

If you are working with unfinished furniture and want to do several large pieces that match, I recommend going to a good paint store and buying the wood stain of your choice. This way, you can be sure that you are staining the wood in a consistent color.

If you are doing a smaller piece, and often you will be, you will find that you can make the most wonderful stains in the world simply by using your old dirty turp and the oil colors from your paint box. For example, I happen to be extremely fond of Permalba Burnt Umber: the color creates a beautiful rich stain. I also enjoy staining a plaque with Asphaltum, then darkening the edges with Burnt Umber. You can actually stain in any color or combination of colors in your paint box.

Staining

Follow these steps for staining:

1. Using a rag or sponge brush, wipe the wooden piece to be stained with just a little turp. This will allow the oil color to flow on smoothly.

2. Mix oil color and turp together on a palette or in a small bowl. The proportions aren't particularly important. If you want a darker stain, use more oil and less turp; a lighter stain requires more turp and less pigment.

3-1. Wipe or brush the stain onto the wood.

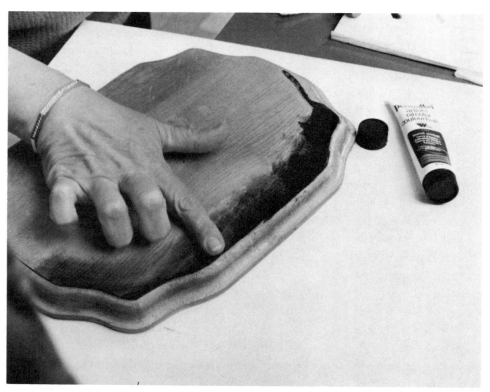

3-2. Rub the Burnt Umber into the wood.

3. Wipe or brush the stain onto the wood. (See figure 3-1).

4. Wipe the stain off, using soft rags or towels.

5. You may wish to darken the edges. To do this apply a small amount of Burnt Umber all the way around the top or outer edge of the board. Using a circular motion, rub the Burnt Umber into the wood with your finger (figure 3-2). Blend the darkened edge into the rest of the stain by rubbing in a circular motion with a dry rag or paper towel. Be careful not to work all the dark away from the outer edge. It is important not to have a ring in the center. You must have a soft, gentle blend from the light in the center to the dark edge.

Sealing

It is necessary to seal a wooden piece. If you are using Priscilla Hauser Wood Sealer (see Sources), this sealer may be applied with a sponge brush directly over the wet oil stain. It will take about two hours for the sealer to dry. The piece should be allowed to dry in a warm room, and there should be excellent air circulation within the room.

If you are using another type of wood sealer, allow the oil stain to dry completely before applying the sealer. After the sealer is dry, a light sanding will be required, as sealing the wood causes the soft grain in the wood to lift.

I would like to share a neat little trick with you that is easy and very effective. I call it "brown paper bagging." Instead of using sandpaper for sanding after a surface has been sealed, take a piece of a brown paper grocery bag and sand with that. Press down hard and be sure there is no printing on the piece of bag that you are going to sand with. Otherwise, the ink will come off on your object. The brown paper bag doesn't actually sand, but it does smooth the surface on which you are going to paint very beautifully and is less trouble than sandpaper. It often does a better job than sandpaper as well.

Pickling

"Pickling" as it applies to raw wood, means staining the wood white. Today, pickling raw wood is very popular.

Even wooden floors are pickled. It gives a wonderful, soft white effect.

The term "pickling" evolves from the white brine look that appears inside old pickle barrels. Pickling is very easy and can be done with either oils or acrylics.

When using oils:

1. Wipe the raw wood with a little turp, just as if you are going to stain it.

2. Using a sponge brush or rag, apply thinned (to desired effect) Permalba White.

3. Wipe the surface with a soft rag, removing enough of the white to allow the grain of the wood to show through. If you are pickling a small piece of furniture, such as a trunk, pickle only one section at a time.

4. Allow the white stain to dry thoroughly. This may take several days, as white is slow to dry.

5. After it dries, rub firmly with a piece of brown paper bag to smooth the wood grain.

6. To seal, you may spray with a number of light coats of clear acrylic spray or apply one coat of water-base varnish. It may be necessary to rub with a brown paper bag once again if the wood grain continues to lift.

I think you will enjoy the pickled effect; it is perfectly beautiful.

To pickle with white acrylic paint or gesso:

1. Dampen the wood with just a little water. Be careful not to use too much—you don't want to warp the surface.

2. With a rag or sponge brush, wipe on (to the desired effect) white acrylic paint or gesso.

3. You may want to apply a second or even a third coat to achieve a whiter finish.

4. After this has dried, "brown paper bag" the project.

5. Seal with many light coats of clear acrylic spray or one coat of water-base varnish.

Two of the projects in this book were pickled, the rose trunk and the poppy trunk. (See color photographs.)

Basecoating

If you are going to paint the wooden piece, you have a number of choices, as there are many different types of paints available. There are acrylic basecoats that are water soluble, oil-base enamels whose solvent is turpentine, spray paints, lacquer-base paints, and so on.

Paints also come in a variety of finishes—high-gloss, semigloss, and flat. I do not like to work on a high-gloss surface—it is too slick and makes blending difficult. A good semigloss surface is fine. A flat surface is generally too flat and will often require some type of sealing before decorating.

I prefer to use acrylic basecoats. These wonderful paints are available in a wide variety of colors. They clean up with water and they dry rapidly. I seldom seal raw wood before applying a basecoat color, as some sealers will make the wood so slick that the paint will not adhere to it. Adhesion is better if the paint is applied to the raw wood.

To apply an acrylic basecoat:

1. Sand if necessary.
2. Using a sponge brush, brush on the desired acrylic basecoat color. Work quickly, because the paint does dry fast; don't go back over it more than is necessary. Acrylic paint is transparent, and often a second or even a third coat is required, depending upon the colors used. If this is the case, let the first coat dry, then lightly sand. Apply a second coat, then a third coat if needed.
3. Because acrylic basecoat is porous, it is important, before transferring the design and painting, to *seal* the acrylic basecoat surface. This may be done in two ways—with a clear acrylic spray or by the application of a water-base varnish.

Clear acrylic sprays are available at most art and craft stores. If you are going to use a clear acrylic spray, you must mist on eight or ten *light coats*, letting the object dry a few seconds after each coat.

If you are going to seal with a water-base varnish, one coat applied with a sponge brush is all that is necessary. Sealing with a water-base varnish sometimes creates a slick surface. To prevent this, I thin the water-base varnish (for example, three parts of water-base varnish to one part water).

After the surface has been properly sealed and is thoroughly dry, the design may be transferred, and painting may begin.

Antiquing

To antique means to "age." You can do this before or after you have done your decorative painting.

There are many antiquing glazes on the market. My Priscilla Hauser Antiquing Glaze (see Sources) is clear; no oil color is added to it. By using a small portion of clear glaze and adding any color or combination of oil colors to it, you can create outstanding color combinations that are not available in any store.

To do this, stir the glaze thoroughly, then spoon approximately two tablespoons into a disposable container. To this, add about ½ teaspoon of one or more oil colors. For a dirty green color, use ¼ teaspoon Burnt Umber and ¼ teaspoon Leaf Green Medium or Olive Green. For a rich brown, use ½ teaspoon Permalba Burnt Umber, Asphaltum, Raw Umber, or a mixture of these colors. A very dark antiquing glaze is made with ¼ teaspoon Burnt Umber and ¼ teaspoon Black (either Lamp or Ivory). A lovely blue can be created with ⅛ teaspoon Prussian Blue and ½ teaspoon Black.

Mix the tube oil paint and the antiquing glaze together. Be sure to seal the object you are going to antique first. By doing this, you can control the amount of antiquing you leave on or wipe off. In other words, the glaze won't soak into your project.

Brush the glaze on the object to be antiqued. Using a folded soft rag, begin wiping off the antiquing glaze. Continue until the desired effect is achieved. If you remove too much glaze, simply apply more and wipe again.

Different effects can be achieved by wiping with different textures of fabric. Try using terry cloth, cheesecloth, or corduroy. Experimenting is fun and a good learning experience.

Two-color Background

You can give a lovely and professional background to a project by using a combination of two colors of paint or a combination of stain and paint. To combine stain and paint, first stain the wood. Let it dry, then sand it or brown paper bag it.

Transfer an oval (or shape of your choice) to the wood, tracing around the oval with a piece of chalk. Paint the oval with two coats of acrylic basecoat. Let this dry, then seal with many light coats of clear acrylic spray or one coat of thinned-down water-base varnish.

Sand or brown paper bag the surface before transferring the design and painting.

Finishes

There are many different types of varnishes or finishes on the market. It is important that you know how to work with them so that you don't crack, craze, or lift your painting.

When applying an oil-base finish over oil paint, be sure that the paint is not only dry, but cured. Paint can feel dry to the touch, but may not be dry or cured throughout. The time it takes for an oil painting to cure depends on two things—the colors that are used and the thickness of the paint. Colors such as reds and whites are much slower to dry than earth tones, and thick paint will take longer to cure than thin.

A piece will usually be dry enough to varnish in several days, if it has been placed in a warm room where the air circulation is good and the humidity is low.

If you are working with an oil-base varnish, apply three coats, allowing each coat to dry thoroughly. Sand lightly, and apply a final coat.

If a water-base varnish is used as a finish, it is not as important that the oil paint be completely cured. You can apply a water-base varnish over oil paint. The first application of a water-base varnish over oil may separate over the oil paint, but let this dry and apply a second and a third coat. It will work beautifully.

I am often asked how to finish items such as mailboxes, tavern signs, or decorative accessories that will be used out-of-doors. The best way to finish these pieces is to let them dry and cure thoroughly. Then use a marine finish or polyurethane finish. Even then, exposure to the weather will eventually force you to bring them back in, sand them, and give them another finish.

Lining a Trunk

Lining a trunk, which you can do beautifully and easily, adds to the overall effect you are creating with your painting.

Padded Lining

Now that your trunk is all painted and beautiful on the outside, let's make the inside just as lovely.

First, choose a fabric to complement the outside of the trunk. For example, a child's trunk could be lined in a children's print. A trunk with a sentimental motif could be done in a quilted cotton fabric in a solid or print. The most popular materials used are velveteen, corduroy, cotton, and cotton blends. Let your imagination go to work and have fun.

Supplies. You will need the following:

fabric (the size of the trunk will determine the amount required)
trim
light cardboard or poster board
pencil or tailor's chalk
glue
scissors
ruler
cotton or polyester quilt batting
decorative tacks
ribbon
eyelet
lace

Trunk Tray. If you plan to use the tray, paint the tray supports, as the lining will not cover them. Let them dry.

Trunk Bottom. Follow these steps:

1. Trunk linings are put in by sections. For instance, the bottom of the trunk will have five sections—right-hand side, left-hand side, front, back, and bottom. If the trunk tray is to be used, the sides of the trunk will be lined with two pieces, one above and one below the tray support. Do not cover the support itself.

2. Measure all edges of each section of the trunk. Subtract ¼ inch (more if a heavy fabric such as corduroy is to be used) from the actual measure-

ments to allow for material fold-over. Now cut a pattern from light cardboard or poster board from your measurements.

3. If you plan to pad the trunk lining, cut cotton or polyester quilt batting a bit smaller than the cardboard pattern and glue the padding to the right side of the pattern.

4. Place the fabric wrongside-up on a large flat surface. Be sure the fabric grain or pattern is straight and going the same way for all sections. Then place the pattern rightside-down on the fabric. Outline the pattern with a pencil or tailor's chalk.

5. Allow ¾ inch to 1 inch on each side of the chalk pattern for fabric fold-over and cut out the fabric.

6. Place the fabric on a flat surface wrongside-up. Lay the cardboard pattern padded side down inside the chalked lines on the back of the fabric. Spread glue on the edges of the cardboard; then carefully fold the fabric over the edges of the cardboard. *Note: do not glue the bottom fabric allowance. This will later be glued to the bottom of the trunk.* Smooth out the folded edges all the way to the corners. Press the material together, forming a point at each corner. Now lay your scissors flat on the cardboard, with the point of the excess fabric between the blades, and cut. This leaves a very neat corner.

7. As each section is completed, place it in the trunk to be sure it fits. If it is too tight, correct it before the glue dries. Just peel the fabric back, trim the cardboard, then reglue the fabric.

8. When all sections of the trunk bottom have been covered and checked for proper fit, glue the sections in place. Apply glue to the trunk, one section at a time. Start with the front; glue that section in place and glue the bottom inch of fabric allowance to the floor of the trunk. This makes a neater fit when the bottom section is put in. Continue around the trunk, gluing the bottom section in last.

9. If the metal arm that supports the lid is to be used, cut a semicircle out of the cardboard pattern so that the arm will have room to fold when the lid is closed. If the support is missing, choose a pretty gold braid or chain. Be sure to fasten this securely to the side of the trunk before the lining is glued in place.

10. A staple gun or tacks may be used at the top

edge of the trunk lining to ensure longer wear. Cover the staples or tacks with a decorative trim or the same braid used for the supports. Decorative tacks may also be used.

11. Trim with lace, eyelet, and ribbons as desired.

Trunk Lid. The lid of the trunk is lined in the same manner. When lining a curved lid, be sure the cardboard pattern will fit into the curve without breaking sharply. If this happens, pad the curve with cotton to the point where the cardboard will fit smoothly.

To tuft the lid, mark the back of the cardboard with the pattern you have chosen. Pad the lid a bit thicker than the bottom of the trunk; then glue the fabric in place. Using strong yarn or thread, push a needle through the cardboard, padding, and fabric. Taking a small stitch, go back through the fabric, padding, and cardboard, leaving enough thread ends to tie securely. It is a good idea to pull these thread ends through a flat button before tying them. This keeps the thread from cutting through the cardboard. Decorative beads or buttons can also be caught in the stitch on the right side of the fabric for an added touch.

When tufting is complete, glue the sides of the lid in place. Glue the tufted lid in last.

Unpadded Lining

You may line a trunk by gluing the fabric directly to the inside surface. It is less elegant, of course, but it can be quite lovely.

1. Measure the inside back and front of the trunk.

2. Cut your material 3 inches longer than the length and 1½ inches longer than the height measurement.

3. Measure the ends of the trunk. Cut your material 1¼ inches smaller than the actual width measurement and 1½ inches longer than the height measurement.

4. Cut a piece of cardboard or poster board ¼ inch smaller on all sides than the bottom of the trunk. Cut a piece of fabric 2 inches larger than the cardboard (1 inch larger on all sides of the cardboard).

5. Dilute craft glue with an equal amount of water.

6. Apply this solution to the inside back of the trunk and around 1½ inches on the ends of the trunk.

7. Apply the fabric to the glue, aligning the center of the fabric to the center back of the trunk and placing the fabric even with the top. Smooth in all directions from the center of the panel. Use your fingers or a table knife to push the fabric into the corners.

8. Glue the inside front panel in the same way.

9. Apply diluted glue on the inside ends of the trunk, also covering the fabric that has extended from the front and back panels. Push the fabric into place so that it is even with the top and the lap-over on the bottom.

10. Place the bottom fabric wrongside-up on the table. Lay the cardboard on top of it. Apply full-strength glue all around the cardboard. Pull the fabric over the sides and ends of the cardboard to secure the fabric on the cardboard. Be sure to pull the fabric straight so that no wrinkles appear. Slide the cardboard into the trunk with the fabric-side up.

11. Trim with lace, ribbons, or braid as desired.

12. The lid of the trunk may be lined in the same manner or it may be painted in a contrasting or coordinating color.

4 Folk Art

In October 1983 I was teaching in my Tulsa Studio when I was called to the phone. It was Jacques Zuidema (the Netherlands national floral painter), who extended an invitation to me that changed my life and made me rethink my definitions of what folk art painting is.

I had been asked to represent the United States, along with ten artists from ten other countries, all invited to Amsterdam to make a presentation to His Royal Highness Prince Bernhard of the Netherlands (figure 4-1). At that time, Prince Bernhard was president of the Worldwide Wildlife Federation. Greeting cards were published from the work that we presented to the Prince to raise money for the Federation.

This was my first trip to Europe, and although I had studied and painted various forms of folk art for many years, I couldn't believe how little I knew about the

4-1. Priscilla Hauser with Prince Bernhard of the Netherlands.

numerous styles of European folk art. Every European country has its own form of folk art. Each country not only has its own style, but many styles. Different districts within each country have styles of folk art individual to that district.

A whole series of lessons could be written on the different folk arts of European countries. From Austria we have Tyrolean painting and from Norway, Rosemaling, which includes styles from Telemark, Halingdahl, Rougland, and other areas. From Germany comes Bauernmalerei, which translates as "farmer painting." The Netherlands brings us sixteenth-century Dutch Assendelfter painting and the beautiful colors and styles of Henderlopen and others. French folk art is so beautiful and detailed it made me want to stay in France and study it. The Swiss Baroque style is gorgeous . . . and I could go on and on.

I learned there were, and still are today, two types of folk artists:

• The professional folk artist who makes a living painting furniture, churches, buildings, and accessories. This work is often very detailed and beautiful.
• The nonprofessional folk artist whose work may be quite primitive by comparison.

Most early European folk art was done using egg temperas or oils. Today we also have acrylics, which are water based and dry rapidly. You might enjoy trying some folk art painting in acrylics as well.

Brush-stroke work is part of most European folk art designs. Remember, when you are doing brush-stroke work, that the consistency of your paint must be extremely thin and loose. When you are blending, the paint must be much thicker in consistency. I must urge you to practice your brush strokes, for they will enrich your painting capability dramatically.

To define folk art painting is not easy. One might say it is the painting of the people, the land, the flowers, the period, the religion. It can be simple, yet charming; some of it is very primitive and some unbelievably elegant.

My style of American folk art is created by borrowing a little from the folk art styles of many different countries. The colors I use in my designs can be in any combination—there are no set rules. A heart doesn't have to be red; it can be white, it can be blue, it can be yellow. Tulips can be any combination of colors, and stylized leaves don't always have to be green.

Colors

The choice of colors, as I have said before, is yours. There are no set rules. The colors should coordinate with the colors of the background on which you are painting and should also look well with the colors in the room where you plan to use the painting.

You will find my worksheet for folk art flowers, forms, hearts, and leaves on the brush-stroke worksheet (W-2). Photographs of projects—a dining chair, a tavern sign, and a wine rack—can be seen in C-1, C-2, and C-3. Patterns for these projects are figures 13-1, 13-2, and 13-3.

Brushes

Your brush size will depend upon the size of your design.

Painting

The painting techniques used for the European folk art designs are up to you. You have learned the brush strokes and have learned how to dry-brush blend earlier in this book.

Comma strokes may be painted with round red-sable watercolor brushes or the flat red-sable brushes. The stroke work should be done very neatly and carefully and as *consistently* are possible.

Remember that when you do brush-stroke work, the paint must be of a thin, loose, almost bird-blessing consistency, and when you dry-brush blend the colors together, the heart for example, the paint must be of a thicker consistency or overblending will take place. Fine detail and line work should be done with a #1 liner brush and the paint consistency should be that of ink.

Now, put all the painting knowledge together that you have learned from the earlier pages of this book, study my color worksheets, and go for it. You will love it.

5 Leaves

Have you heard that leaves are hard? Have you heard people say they don't like to paint them? Well, that is silly. They are not hard. Yes, they take practice and they take discipline, but I have students who absolutely love to paint leaves once they have learned how to do it.

Leaves are like the perfect frame on a beautiful painting; they frame the subject matter. They shouldn't be so busy that they draw away from the subject matter; rather, they should enhance and add to it.

There are many different types of leaves and just as many ways to paint them.

Before you actually begin to paint them, there are things you need to understand about leaves in general.

Lighting

In the world of decorative painting, unlike other methods of painting, we do not paint with an established light source. In other words, we don't say "here's our design, and the light is entering from the right side."

Please be aware of the fact that you are decorating objects (for example, the outside of a milk can or the floor of a tray).

Instead of envisioning a light source, simply remember that objects will be light in the front, dark in the back, and a medium value in the middle. In other words, anything closer to the front will be lighter; things that are to the back will be darker.

When painting leaves, number the leaves on the design, breaking them into groups of three. Leaves that are the farthest to the back and darkest will be #1; leaves that are in the middle of the design will be #2; and those that are the closest to the front of the design will be #3—they are the lightest leaves.

Contrast Between Leaves

It is extremely important when painting leaves to paint with *contrast* between the three values. In order to achieve this, I use three shades of Leaf Green. Leaf Green Dark is used for the #1 or dark-value leaves; Leaf Green Medium for the #2 or medium-value leaves; and Leaf Green Light for the #3 or lightest leaves.

You may mix the three values of green yourself or use colors that are premixed for you. The latter, in my opinion, is an easier way to go. However, if you want to be a purist and mix your colors, here is what to do:
- Begin with medium-value leaves. For Leaf Green Medium, mix Cadmium Yellow Medium with just a touch of Lamp Black and a tiny touch of Prussian Blue.
- To mix Leaf Green Dark, take a portion of the Leaf Green Medium that you have mixed and add a good deal of Lamp Black.
- For Leaf Green Light, mix equal amounts of Leaf Green Medium, Permalba White, and Yellow Citron.

Additional Colors Used in Leaves

Now that your three shades of Leaf Green have been established, I would like to give you the additional colors used in leaves.

For a dark-value leaf, the following colors are used: Burnt Umber, Leaf Green Dark, and Ice Blue. Sometimes, depending upon the subject matter that I am painting, I will also use a touch of Burnt Sienna in the base or bottom of my dark-value leaf.

For a medium-value leaf, the colors used are: Leaf Green Medium, Burnt Umber, Permalba White, Yellow Citron, Cadmium Yellow Medium, and Ice Blue if desired.

For a light-value leaf, the appropriate colors are: a limited amount of Burnt Umber, Leaf Green Light, Cadmium Yellow Light, Permalba White, and a little Ice Blue if desired.

When Painting Leaves

Keep these tips in mind:

- The paint for "blocking in" the strokes should be slightly thinner than the paint you add to the center for blending. In order to do this, you must control the consistency, which is discussed in chapter 1. Remember that brush-stroke work requires that the paint be a little thinner; dry-brush blending requires the paint to be thicker. If your paint is too thin when you blend, you will overblend and make mud.
- Don't blend too long. This is hard for everybody to learn. You have to know when to stop before overblending takes place.
- Don't wipe too much paint off on your rag. Leave some paint on the leaf to blend.
- Don't be afraid to turn your work. Find the position that is most comfortable for you to use in painting.
- Don't be afraid to add any color you desire in the center of the leaf. Remember that dark-value leaves must be dark and light-value leaves must be light. Often, when I am painting a strawberry or an iris, I will add a touch of the main subject color to the base or bottom of my leaf so that the main subject color then reflects in the leaf.

Dry-Brush Blend Leaf

I am going to give you complete step-by-step instructions for painting a middle-value brush stroke dry-brush blend leaf. You will find this leaf painted stroke by stroke on the color worksheet (W-1). On this worksheet, you will also find the setup for a dark-value leaf and a light-value leaf.

Colors

See the discussion on page 24 and above.

Brushes

The size of the brush you use will depend on the size of the leaf that you are painting. Small leaves require small brushes; large leaves require large brushes. This is why it is very important that you eventually build your collection of those beautiful red-sable brushes to include every other size from a #00 red-sable flat through a #16 or even #20 red-sable flat.

Painting

Put all the needed colors on your palette and mix the paint to a thick, creamy consistency. Remember that when doing brush-stroke work, you must control the consistency, so that for the actual blocking-in, you are touching your turp, then blotting on the soft absorbent rag so that the paint is just a little thinner for the brush-stroke part only. Work as follows:

1. Double load your flat sable brush with Leaf Green Medium and Burnt Umber. Blend on your palette to soften the color. Darken at the base or bottom of the leaf. This creates a shadow. (There is always a shadow where a leaf goes under another leaf or under a fruit or flower.)

2. Apply the first stroke as shown on the color worksheet (W-1). *Notice that the first stroke pulls right down into the shadow.*

3. Place a second stroke above the first stroke.

4. The third stroke forms the center of the leaf. Stand the brush on its flat edge with the Burnt Umber side pointing straight up; pull toward you, letting the brush roll to the left. Study the color worksheet.

5. Clean the brush and double load it with Leaf Green Medium and White. Paint a commalike stroke opposite the second stroke.

6. Paint a commalike stroke opposite the first stroke; the white will be on the outside edge.

7. You have now blocked in a leaf using the basic brush strokes. Wipe your brush and add the colors to the center of the leaf. This is a medium-value leaf, so you will add more Leaf Green Medium, Cadmium Yellow Medium, and Yellow Citron.

8. Wipe the brush and lightly blend the colors around in a circle.

9. Come back to the base of the leaf and restroke lightly out into each of the original strokes you have made. Please study the color worksheet to see how this is done. Wipe the brush each time.

10. Stroke lightly from the outside edge back toward the base of the leaf. Again, I urge you to study the color worksheet.

11. Accent the edges of the leaf. I usually use Ice Blue for my accent color, although other colors may be used if desired. An accent should be placed only when it is needed. For example, when one dark edge is on top of another dark edge, the two dark edges side by side won't show up. We can use an accent stroke on the top leaf to make the top edge visible in contrast to the shadow underneath it. Again, you can study this example on the worksheet.

To apply the accent, pick up a little Ice Blue. Then, come right out over the edge of the stroke you are placing the accent on, touch, pull, and lift quickly. This takes a little practice, but it is that special touch that really makes your work lovely.

More Painting Tips

- The basic brush stroke dry-brush blend leaf is usually a five-stroke leaf, so your brush must be large enough to block in the leaf completely in five strokes. The only exception to this rule is when you are painting a very long slender leaf, such as a pear or peach leaf; in such cases, seven and only seven strokes should be used.
- Block the leaf in clockwise. A student of mine once said that when painting a five-stroke leaf, it helped her to think of a clock. She placed the first stroke at about eight o'clock, the next stroke at ten o'clock, the center stroke at noon, the fourth stroke at two o'clock, and the fifth stroke at four o'clock. I hope this is helpful to you.
- This technique adapts to almost any shape leaf, be it short and fat or long and slender.

When I say that you have to paint at least 50 of these leaves to get started and 100 to be good, don't throw this book down and go curl up in a corner. Remember—doing anything well takes nothing more than practice and self-discipline. If you want to do it, you can. I know you want

to do it or you wouldn't have bought this book. So get busy, pay your dues, and see what joy painting will bring you.

Veining a Leaf

There are many ways to vein a leaf, but I want to keep this simple. Therefore, paint the vein using the flat edge of the flat brush or the point of your liner brush. The paint must have a very thin, almost inklike consistency. You don't want the vein to detract from the leaf but to add to it gently. The vein should be painted in the darkest shading color used in the leaf, which in this case is Burnt Umber. It is generally a curved, rather than a straight line; it starts at the bottom and doesn't quite reach the top.

Scribble Leaf

The scribble leaf is not difficult to paint but also requires the knowledge of double loading and the use of proper paint consistency.

Scribble leaves are jagged in shape. They are fun to paint because you "scribble" on the edges of the leaf with the edge of a flat brush, just like you used to scribble with a pencil when you were a child.

Some jagged-edge leaves are what we call sectioned leaves. In other words, there may be three, five, or more sections in one leaf. The leaf that I have painted on the color worksheet (W-1) is a sectioned leaf, but I want you to be aware of the fact that not all jagged-edge leaves are sectioned. Sometimes a jagged-edge leaf can have only one dark side and one light side. Study the leaves in each design that you are going to paint. Decide on the placement of light and dark, as well as on the number of sections involved, *before* you begin to paint the leaf.

The scribble leaf is painted in dark, medium, and light values, using the same combinations of colors that we have used in the other leaves.

Colors

The colors most commonly used to paint scribble leaves are: Leaf Green Medium, Burnt Umber, Burnt Sienna,

Prussian Blue, Permalba White, Ice Blue, Yellow Citron, and Cadmium Yellow Medium.

Brushes

Once again, the brush size will depend upon the size of the leaf you are painting. On the color worksheet, I have used a #6 to scribble in the edges of the leaves and a #8 or #10 for blending the center.

Painting

Cream the needed leaf colors to the consistency of soft butter. Then:

1. Double load the flat brush with the Leaf Green Medium and Burnt Umber. Blend on the palette to soften the color.

2. Darken at the base or bottom of the leaf; a little Burnt Sienna and/or Prussian Blue may be added on the dark side of the brush if desired.

3. Begin to scribble carefully in a back-and-forth motion up the dark side of the first section of the leaf.

4. Clean the brush and load it with the Leaf Green Medium and Permalba White or Ice Blue. Scribble down the light side.

5. Refill the brush with the Leaf Green Medium and the Burnt Umber and scribble up the dark side of the second section.

6. Clean the brush, double load it with the Leaf Green Medium and the White, and scribble down the light section. Notice, on the color worksheet, that I roll around the corners of the turn between sections with almost a "U" stroke.

7. Scribble in the third section of the leaf with the Leaf Green Medium and White on both sides of the section. (Remember this is the light side of the leaf.)

8. Wipe the brush and add more Leaf Green Medium, a little Yellow Citron, and some Cadmium Yellow Medium to the center of the leaf. Wipe the brush or pick up a larger brush; put some Leaf Green Medium paint in it, wipe it on the rag, then begin to blend lightly.

9. You will probably find it necessary to rescribble the edges of the leaves upon completion to tie the blending and the edges together.

10. If desired, vein the leaf using the flat edge of the flat brush or the point of your #1 liner. Use thin paint for the vein and keep the vein small and simple. You don't want the leaf to appear busier than it is.

6 Forget-me-nots

I had never seen forget-me-nots except in photographs until I traveled to Europe. In the fields of France, I found these tiny, delicate flowers in blues, pinks, and whites. They are just gorgeous. Their leaves are simple blade or basic leaves. The little flowers have five petals.

I like to use them for decorating small pieces, such as the pencil box, vanity mirror, potpourri box, and piano music box shown in C-4, C-5, C-6, and C-7 in the color section. (They also lend themselves well in other designs as fillers.) For patterns for each of these small projects, see figures 13-4, 13-5, 13-6, and 13-7.

Study the forget-me-nots on the color worksheet (W-3). I urge you to be careful and take your time. They are not difficult to paint, but they must not be rushed.

Colors

For the blue forget-me-nots, make a blue mixture by adding a touch of Prussian Blue to Permalba White.

The colors needed are: Prussian Blue, Permalba White, Cadmium Yellow Light, Lamp Black, and, if desired, a touch of Mauve.

Brushes

You will need very small, flat, red-sable brushes—a #1 or #2, and your #1 liner or scroll brush.

Painting

Cream the colors to a relatively thin consistency. The Permalba White, in particular, should have an extremely thin, bird-blessing consistency. Then follow these steps:

1. Undercoat the small areas of the flowers with the desired colors. On the worksheet, I used a very small amount of Prussian Blue and a little Mauve. Blend these two colors together.

2. Wipe the brush. Then, using a very small flat brush and very thin paint, paint the dark-value five-petaled flowers all over the area, including the outside edge and the flower area. Examine the worksheet.

3. Clean the brush and fill it with the thin, light blue mixture. Paint medium-value flowers on top of the dark-value flowers, staggered over the bunch.

4. Clean the brush again and fill it with the thin Permalba White. Add just a few very white flowers on top of the medium-value flowers.

Please note that the flower petals are formed with comma strokes, starting on the outside edge of each petal and stroking in toward the center.

Centers

The centers are very easy to paint:

1. Using your #1 liner brush and very thin Cadmium Yellow Light, paint a tiny dot of the yellow mixture in each center.

2. Apply a tinier dot of very thin Lamp Black right on top of the yellow.

7 Daisies

If there is anything more exciting than looking, touching, and smelling flowers, it is being able to paint them. And you *can* paint them—beautifully. I combined daisies with chrysanthemums in three projects, which you can see in the color section—a footstool (C-11), a music box (C-12), and a camelback trunk (C-13). (Patterns for these projects are figures 13-11, 13-12, and 13-13.)

I will never tire of teaching or painting daisies. They are just beautiful! They can be done in so many different ways. Daisies can be painted using a flat brush or a round brush. They can be painted in a multitude of color combinations. Don't be afraid to experiment. Try the colors you'd really like for daisies. Sometimes the color combinations will work out beautifully; other times you will find them less attractive than you had imagined. Don't despair; if something doesn't work, try again.

Read and then reread my instructions for painting daisies. Then take brush in hand, making sure that your paint is of the proper consistency.

Lay a sheet of tracing paper or acetate over my step-by-step worksheet (W-4) and go for it! I want you to practice the petal strokes themselves. (These strokes are actually variations of comma strokes and "S" strokes.) Begin stroking at the outside edge of the petal, lifting slightly as you come in toward the center. Practice these strokes many times before you actually paint a daisy on an object.

There are many varieties of daisies, and the shapes of the petals can vary dramatically. By varying the shape and size of your brush strokes, you will find that you can create any variety you desire.

Almost all daisies require two coats of paint: an undercoat, which is a color, and a top coat, which is Permalba White whipped with odorless turp to the consistency of whipped cream, so that the paint actually holds peaks. As I have tried to stress, the consistency of the paint is extremely important. When stroking daisy petals, the top coat must be very loose, so that it flows evenly and easily from the hairs of the brush. The undercoat color should be very thin—almost a wash in consistency. If you use too much color underneath the daisy, this color will bleed through, and the white will not be attractive.

In painting a group of daisies, the daisies to the back of the design should be darker and those in front should be lighter. Therefore, more of the undercoat color should be used on the darker daisies, less on the lighter daisies. You will see this demonstrated on my color worksheet.

One of my favorite undercoat colors for the daisies is a marvelous color called Paynes Gray. This is a very versatile color. It can create the look of a white daisy, yet when used on a blue background, one would almost think the daisies were blue. On a black background, the Paynes Gray undercoat is simply stunning. However, remember that you can choose any undercoat color for a daisy.

Now gather all the needed supplies together and paint daisies!

Colors

Daisies require the following colors: Paynes Gray or Ivory Black, Permalba White, Cadmium Yellow Medium, Burnt Sienna, Burnt Umber, and Cadmium Red Light.

Brushes

The size of your fine red-sable brush depends entirely on the size of the daisy petal you are painting. For practicing the daisy I have painted on the color worksheet, I recommend a #6 flat red-sable brush and a #1 liner or scroll brush.

Painting

1. Fill your #6 flat red-sable brush with very thin Paynes Gray or Ivory Black. Paint commalike strokes, beginning at the outside edge of the petals and pulling in toward the center, lifting slightly.

2. Clean your brush in turp; then blot it on your soft absorbent rag or towel.

3. Fill the brush completely with Permalba White, whipped to the consistency of whipped cream.

4. Put your brush down just beyond the end of the Paynes Gray and restroke the petal completely, covering the Paynes Gray with the white. If you want the petal to be darker, do not wipe the brush and do not pick up more white. If you want the petal to be lighter, wipe the brush and fill it with white paint each time you stroke. Be sure you paint all the white petals while the Paynes Gray undercoat is wet—otherwise there will be no bleed-through or shading of the petals.

Daisy Center

The technique for painting the daisy center is as follows:

1. Using a #6 or smaller flat red-sable brush, neatly and carefully paint the daisy center with Cadmium Yellow Medium. Leave a little empty space for shading down the left side and across the bottom of the center.

2. Double load your small flat brush with Cadmium Yellow Medium and Burnt Sienna. Blend on your palette to soften the color. With the Burnt Sienna on the outside, carefully shade down the left side and across the bottom of the daisy center. Wipe your brush; pat and blend. Be sure you have excellent contrast between the Yellow and the Sienna—this will really make the daisy live.

3. Fill a #1 liner with very thin, inklike Burnt Umber and neatly apply dots around the center of the daisy. Please study the color worksheet to see the placement of the dots. Notice that some of the dots actually fall out onto the petals, and others come slightly into the center. Generally, I use more Umber dots than any other color. Start with Umber dots; then add Permalba White dots and just a few dots of Cadmium Red Light.

Daisy Leaf

The leaf I generally use for the daisy is the basic brush stroke dry-brush blend leaf. However, the scribble leaf creates a lovely daisy leaf as well.

Remember to paint with contrast between leaves. Leaves to the back of the design are generally darker, those to the front of the design are lighter.

8 Strawberries

Pick up your paint brush and paint strawberries with me, but plan to spend some time doing so. The strawberry itself is just as easy as can be, but the details of the seeds and the bracts that sit on top of the strawberry's head will slow you down a bit.

Strawberries are delicious to eat and beautiful to paint. They are one of my favorite things, and they work beautifully with daisies. They lend themselves well to all types of designs using fruit as well as flowers.

Before you start, take a look at the strawberries painted on the dining chair (C-8), the crate (C-9), and the clock (C-10). Patterns for these can be found in figures 13-8, 13-9, and 13-10.

Now settle down in a soft, comfortable chair, read and reread my instructions, and follow along on the step-by-step color worksheet (W-9) that I have provided for you. After you have studied the lesson carefully, get out your paints. Cream them to the proper consistency and let's paint strawberries!

Colors

Strawberries can be painted in a number of different color combinations, from the very ripe red berry to the very unripe, almost white and yellow-green berry.

The following colors may be used: Permalba White, Cadmium Red Light, Cadmium Red Medium, Burnt Alizarin, Yellow Citron or Leaf Green Light, Cadmium Orange, and Ice Blue.

For the seeds, use Cadmium Yellow Light and Lamp Black.

For the bracts, use Leaf Green Light or Medium, Burnt Umber, Permalba White, and Yellow Citron.

Brushes

The size of your red-sable brushes will depend on the size of the strawberry that you are painting. Generally, the smaller sizes of brushes are used. The little Grape Blender manufactured for me by Robert Simmons, Inc., is a won-derful little tool for the final light blending of strawberries. Be careful when you use this little brush that you don't overblend. Use a flat red-sable brush for the bracts.

A #1 liner or scroll brush is needed for applying the seeds.

Painting

Cream the oil colors for the berry to a soft, buttery consistency. I am providing instructions for a medium-value berry.

1. Paint the center of the berry in Permalba White.

2. Apply Cadmium Red Light around the White.

3. Wipe your brush and double load it with the Burnt Alizarin and Cadmium Red Light. Blend on the palette to soften the color. Shade the left (or dark) side of the berry. The Burnt Alizarin will be on the outside.

4. Wipe the brush and double load the brush with the dirty brush and Cadmium Orange. Blend on the palette to soften the color. Shade the right (or light) side of the berry. Wipe the brush and double load with the dirty brush and a little Ice Blue, bringing the Ice Blue around the dark side of the berry, as shown on the color worksheet (W-9). This is what we call a "secondary reflection." It makes the strawberry look like it continues around on the dark side.

5. Wipe the brush or pick up a larger flat brush, put some paint in it, and wipe it off so that you are not putting a clean brush down on the berry. Begin to dry-brush blend the berry lightly, stroking from the top to the bottom and from the bottom to the top.

6. Cross blend if necessary.

7. Go back and lightly blend, following the natural curve of the berry. The little Grape Blender may be used for final blending if desired, but don't overdo it.

The Seeds

Work on the seeds as follows:

1. The seeds *curve* with the shape of the strawberry. Students often put strawberry seeds on berries so that they are straight up and down, but this is not natural at all. If you do this, it will look like it is raining yellow on your strawberry. Let the seeds curve on the left side, curve on the right side, and be rather straight in the middle. The seeds should always be put on the strawberry while the berry is wet, because they are actually a part of the berry. To apply the seeds, I use my #1 liner brush, a very good pair of glasses so that I can see what I am doing, and very thin Cadmium Yellow Light and Lamp Black paint. Apply the seeds staggered over the wet strawberry, as shown on the color worksheet (W-9).

2. The Lamp Black is optional. It is beautiful if you can see well enough and have a steady enough hand to apply it. It should be applied on the outside edge of each seed; it actually sets the seed down into the berry.

Bracts

The strawberry bracts may be painted after the strawberry is dry. Alternatively, you can clean out the areas by dipping your brush in turp, blotting it on your rag, and then carefully lifting out the areas where the bracts are to be painted.

Blend the paints to a relatively thin, creamy consistency. The bracts are formed using brush strokes, and the paint must flow from the hairs of the brush. Then do the following:

1. Double load a small flat brush with Leaf Green Medium and Burnt Umber. Blend on palette to soften color. Begin by painting "U" strokes around the stem where the base of the bracts all meet, as shown on the color worksheet.

2. With your double-loaded brush, paint an "S" stroke of Burnt Umber and Leaf Green Medium, as shown on the worksheet.

3. Double load the brush with Leaf Green Medium and Permalba White or Ice Blue. Paint a second "S" stroke.

4. Wipe the brush and add a little Yellow Citron to the center of the bract.

5. Wipe the brush and lightly blend.

The bracts are difficult to paint the first time you try them because they are tiny, and they do take time. Paint them neatly, paint them carefully, and once your dues are paid, you will be delighted with the finished result.

The Unripe Strawberry

On the color worksheet, I have painted for you a little strawberry that is not quite ripe. I have used Permalba White, Yellow Citron or Leaf Green Light, Cadmium Red Light, and the tiniest touch of Burnt Alizarin.

Try your own color combinations with strawberries. Color is marvelous, and you will be fascinated with the results.

Undercoating

You will notice on the strawberry worksheet that I undercoated the strawberries very neatly and very carefully. I did this because I was painting on a black or dark background. It is not always necessary to undercoat, but when working on a dark background, you want your colors to be very bright. Undercoating can be a great asset. The undercoating must be very neatly and smoothly done and must be exactly within the lines of the design. Otherwise, it can be more of a hindrance to you than a help, for it will show through and you will not be pleased with the results.

When I undercoat, I use a white acrylic basecoat, which is very smooth and creamy. I use an old red-sable brush that has been washed in soap and water to remove any oil residue from the hairs. Then, working as neatly and smoothly as I can, undercoat the design.

After the first application of the acrylic basecoat is dry, I apply a second and sometimes even third, if needed. It is much better to apply several thin coats of acrylic when undercoating than one coat that is too heavy.

9 Chrysanthemums

Chrysanthemums come in every color combination imaginable. They are very fast to paint if you have control of comma strokes. Chrysanthemums are one of the few flowers that lend themselves well to an Oriental decor. If I have large pieces of furniture to decorate, I will often choose chrysanthemums because they are light, airy, and fast, and they will cover a large area in a relatively short period of time.

I used mums in combination with daisies in three projects—a footstool (C-11), a music box (C-12), and a camelback trunk (C-13). For patterns, see figures 13-11, 13-12, and 13-13.

Chrysanthemum *leaves*, however, are an entirely different story. Until you have paid your dues with leaves and really practiced them, they are going to be slow—but definitely worth the final result.

The petals of the chrysanthemums can be painted with the flat red-sable brush or the round red-sable watercolor brush. I think the round brush creates a more graceful petal. However, the flat brush also lends itself to the lovely comma strokes that form the chrysanthemum.

Don't be afraid to experiment with different color combinations. One of the most frustrating parts of preparing this text for you is the fact that there is not enough room for the many different color combinations I would like to present. Nevertheless, I believe I have provided you with enough ideas and enough basic instructions that you can experiment with the fabulous world of color yourself.

Colors

I have used the following colors on the worksheet (W-5): Cadmium Yellow Light, Cadmium Yellow Medium, Burnt Sienna, and Permalba White.

Brushes

The brushes used on the worksheet are: A #6 or #8 flat red-sable brush for applying the colors; a #1 round red-sable watercolor brush for stroking on the petals. For larger flowers, use larger brushes.

Painting

Cream the oil colors to the consistency of soft butter. Cream the Permalba White to a very, very loose whipped-cream consistency. Once again, I must stress that proper paint consistency is the key. The white must be extremely loose.

If you study my worksheet and the design that I have provided for you, you will see that the chrysanthemum is actually divided into two parts—an upper section, which is almost circular in shape, and the lower petals, which fall down and away from the upper section. After you have prepared your paints, do the following:

1. Apply the colors to the upper section, as shown on the color worksheet. Start with Cadmium Yellow Light on the top of the circle, then Cadmium Yellow Medium, then Burnt Sienna at the bottom. Wipe the flat brush and blend these colors together. Be careful not to overblend.

2. Using your finger or a paint brush, pull or pat some of the Sienna at the bottom of the ball and a little of the Yellows down into the area where the lower petals will be painted. This is an important step, as you want the flower colors underneath those lower petals.

3. Fill the brush of your choice, either round or flat, with the creamy thin Permalba White. Be sure the brush is completely full.

4. On your palette, make a stroke over some wet yellow. This will prevent the pure white from being carried to the top of the flower.

5. Paint two commalike strokes opposite each other at the top of the ball, as seen on the worksheet. Do not wipe your brush; do not pick up more paint.

6. Continue the strokes, staggering them over the entire ball and occasionally making a stroke to the outside of the ball. Again, I urge you to study the color worksheet. Do not pick up more paint unless you absolutely have to, for there is a natural shading and darkening of the petals that takes place as you stroke toward the bottom of the ball. If you must pick up more paint, go ahead and do it, but a lovelier effect will be achieved once you are able to complete the petals with one good fill of the brush.

7. Turn the chrysanthemum upside down.

8. Begin to paint the commas forming the lower petals. Notice that the tails of the commas draw "in" toward the center on both sides of the flower. Be sure that your strokes are large enough. Students often make these strokes too small.

9. Paint a second row of petals staggered in between the first row, but don't paint too many—you want the flower to be airy.

10. Turn the chrysanthemum rightside-up and study it. Fill in with an occasional petal where necessary.

When you are painting a group of chrysanthemums, the mums that are to the back should be darker. Those that are to the front should be lighter. To paint the dark flowers, use more dark colors in the undercoat and try not to pick up extra white on your brush when painting the top petals. For the lighter flowers, use lighter colors in the undercoat. Don't be afraid to overlap strokes when painting a light flower on top of a dark flower. Feel free to pick white up more often when painting lighter petals. This will help keep the top flowers lighter.

Chrysanthemum Leaves

Chrysanthemum leaves are somewhat sectioned leaves, and are rather jagged on the edges. The scribble leaf technique works beautifully for chrysanthemum leaves. Be sure to use a touch of the flower color in the base of an occasional leaf; this will help leaves and flowers compliment each other.

10 Country Animals

The country animals are just darling. What fun for everyone to paint! They will work in many different rooms of the house and in many different situations.

I love to cut the animals out of wood and use them in wreaths, on picnic baskets, and other home accessories. Try cutting them in miniature and gluing them on light switches. You can even make bookmarks out of them. The uses for wooden cutout shapes are endless, and the animals are simple to paint.

Lamb

You can see the country lamb and bunny in five projects: a trunk, two plaques, a wreath, and a picnic basket. (See color photographs in C-14 through C-18 and patterns in figures 13-14 through 13-17.)

Colors

The basic colors are Lamp Black and Permalba White. The collar is Cadmium Yellow Medium shaded with Burnt Sienna. The little heart is Cadmium Red Light.

The colors used in the border are: Cadmium Red Light, Burnt Alizarin, Permalba White, Leaf Green Dark, and Leaf Green Light.

Brushes

The brush sizes will vary with the size of the design. On the worksheet (W-6), the lamb is small, so I have used small flat red-sable brushes in sizes #1, #2, #4, and #6, as well as a #1 liner or scroll brush.

Painting

1. To paint the face and legs use a small flat brush. Neatly apply the Permalba White to the highlight areas of the face and legs, as shown on the worksheet. Wipe the brush and apply the Lamp Black. Wipe the brush again and blend where the white and black meet.

2. Using a larger brush, paint the body of the sheep with Permalba White. Apply just a little Lamp Black shading at the neck area on either side of the ribbon that goes around the neck.

3. Wipe the brush and blend.

4. Using a #4 flat brush, make three-quarter circle strokes just like the half-circle strokes, but larger. Twist the brush around in your fingers to create swirls on the blended head and body. This is a very loose, easy technique that is designed to give the effect of curly wool on the lamb.

5. To paint the tail, just dab on Permalba White.

6. To paint the eye, use a #1 liner brush and very thin Lamp Black. Colorbook-paint the eye carefully. Be sure to add a tiny gleam or highlight of white. This will create the sparkle needed to give the lamb a little personality. You can see this tiny highlight on the color worksheet.

7. To paint the ribbon, use a small flat brush. Neatly paint the ribbon in Cadmium Yellow Medium or the color of your choice. Shade with a little Burnt Sienna, wipe the brush, and blend.

8. The little heart may be colorbook-painted with Cadmium Red Light, or it may be painted in Cadmium Red Light and shaded with just a little bit of Burnt Alizarin, if you desire.

Black Lamb

A little black lamb is adorable. To paint a black lamb, use Lamp Black and Permalba White, as you did for the white lamb, but simply reverse the amount of the two colors.

Bunny

The bunny is painted in much the same manner as the lamb, but the texture of the fur is different, of course.

Colors

The colors needed for the bunny are Permalba White and Lamp Black.

The border colors are: Cadmium Red Light, Burnt Alizarin, Permalba White, Leaf Green Dark, and Leaf Green Light.

Brushes

The brush size will vary with the size of the design you are painting. The brushes needed to paint the actual pattern size are: #2, #8, #12, and #14 or #16 flat red-sable tole brushes and a #1 liner or scroll brush.

Painting

Cream the paint to the consistency of soft butter. Then:

1. Using a #8 flat brush, apply the Permalba White to the sections of the bunny, as shown on the worksheet.

2. Wipe the brush and double load it with the Permalba White and Lamp Black. Blend on the palette to soften the color. Neatly pat on the black in all the dark or shaded areas, as shown on the worksheet.

3. Take a larger flat brush, put some white paint in it, then wipe it out on your soft absorbent rag and lightly blend. If the background color shows through, it is probably because you are not using a light enough touch when you are blending. Often, the background color showing through looks like more shading. If this disturbs you, let the paint dry and apply a second coat.

Painting the Bow. The bow around the bunny's neck is painted with Cadmium Red Light and shaded dark with Burnt Alizarin.

It takes a long time to paint a pretty bow. It is something that should not be rushed, for each little section must be neatly painted and shaded. The paint consistency must be thick.

Painting the Eye. The eye is painted with very thin Lamp Black and the #1 liner brush. A tiny highlight of Permalba White must be applied to create the little gleam in the eye.

Try different color combinations for the country animals. A brown bunny can be painted by adding just a touch of Burnt Umber and Burnt Sienna to Permalba White. This will give you a wonderful chocolate brown. The bunny can then be shaded dark with a mixture of Burnt Umber and Burnt Sienna without the white.

Have fun with the country animals. Cows, chickens, and ducks can all be painted in a similar manner. Don't be afraid to experiment. I think you will really enjoy them.

Color Worksheets and Projects

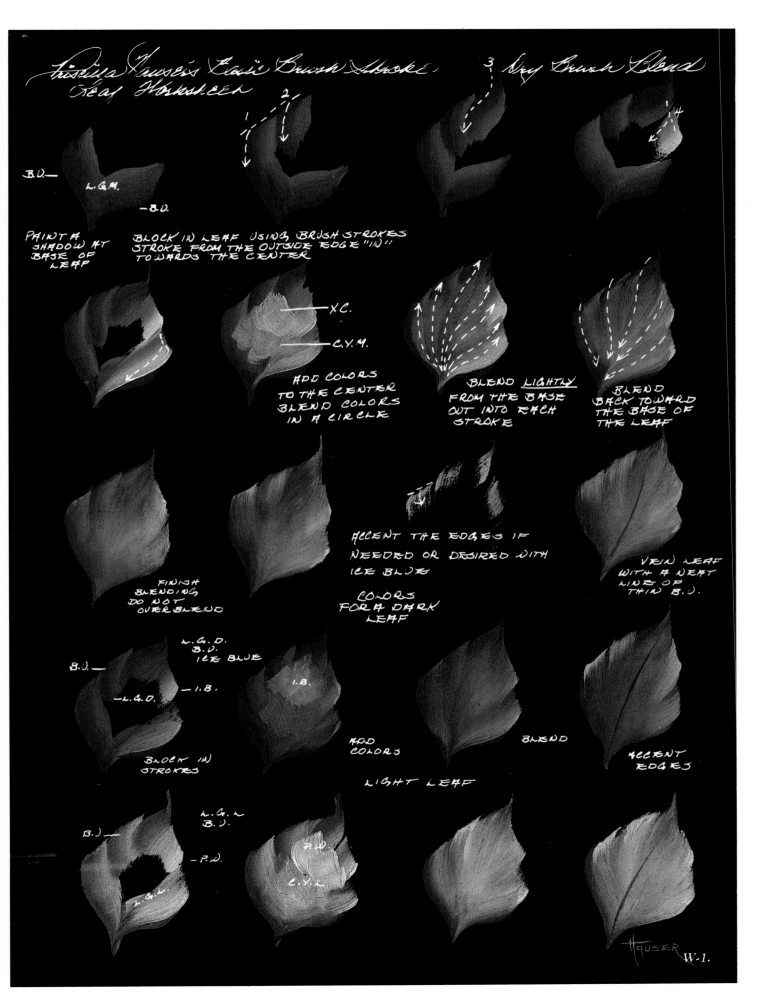

Priscilla Hauser's Basic Brush Stroke   3 Dry Brush Blend
Leaf Worksheet

B.D.—
    L.G.M.
        —B.D.

PAINT A   BLOCK IN LEAF USING BRUSH STROKES
SHADOW AT   STROKE FROM THE OUTSIDE EDGE "IN"
BASE OF   TOWARDS THE CENTER
LEAF

                        — X.C.

                        — C.Y.M.

              ADD COLORS   BLEND LIGHTLY   BLEND
              TO THE CENTER   FROM THE BASE   BACK TOWARD
              BLEND COLORS   OUT INTO EACH   THE BASE OF
              IN A CIRCLE   STROKE   THE LEAF

                        ACCENT THE EDGES IF
                        NEEDED OR DESIRED WITH
                        ICE BLUE

              FINISH   VEIN LEAF
              BLENDING   COLORS   WITH A NEAT
              DO NOT   FOR A DARK   LINE OF
              OVERBLEND   LEAF   THIN B.D.

                    L.G.D.
                    B.D.
                    ICE BLUE
B.D.—
                        —I.B.
      —L.G.D.   I.B.

                    ADD   BLEND   ACCENT
      BLOCK IN   COLORS   EDGES
      STROKES

                    LIGHT LEAF

                    L.G.L.
                    B.D.
B.D.—
                        —P.W.
                    P.W.

                    C.Y.L.

H. Hauser   W-1.

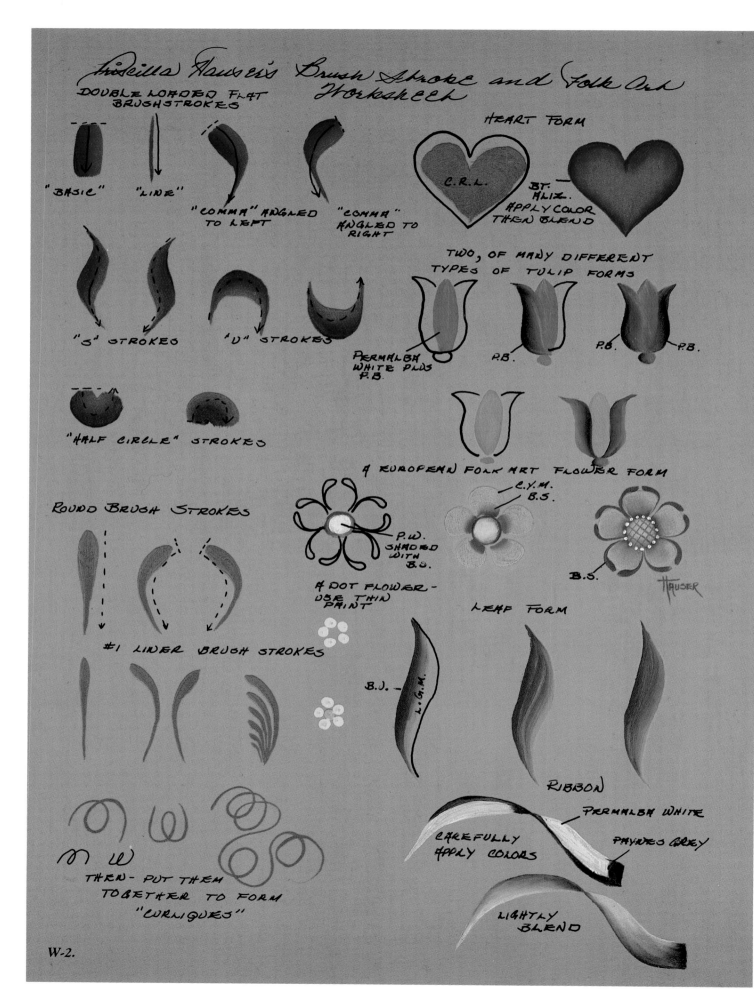

Priscilla Hauser's Brush Stroke and Folk Art Worksheet

DOUBLE LOADED FLAT BRUSHSTROKES

"BASIC" "LINE" "COMMA" ANGLED TO LEFT "COMMA" ANGLED TO RIGHT

HEART FORM

C.R.L. BT. ALIZ.
APPLY COLOR THEN BLEND

"S" STROKES "U" STROKES

TWO, OF MANY DIFFERENT TYPES OF TULIP FORMS

PERMALBA WHITE PLUS P.B. P.B. P.B. P.B.

"HALF CIRCLE" STROKES

A EUROPEAN FOLK ART FLOWER FORM

C.Y.M.
B.S.

ROUND BRUSH STROKES

P.W. SHADED WITH B.S.

A DOT FLOWER- USE THIN PAINT

B.S.

#1 LINER BRUSH STROKES

LEAF FORM

B.J. L.G.M.

RIBBON

PERMALBA WHITE

PAYNES GREY

CAREFULLY APPLY COLORS

THEN - PUT THEM TOGETHER TO FORM "CURLIQUES"

LIGHTLY BLEND

HAUSER

W-2.

C-1.

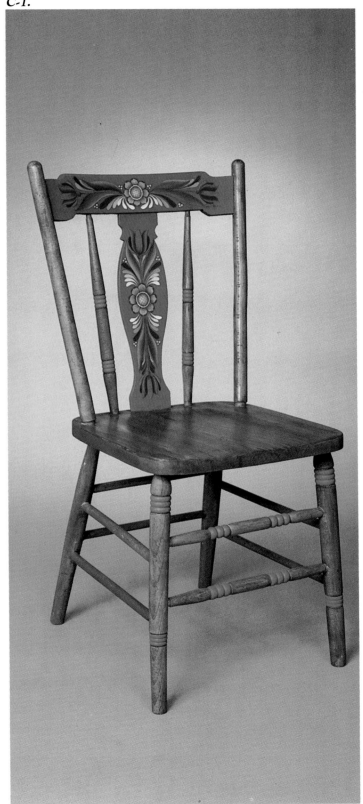

C-2.

C-3.

Priscilla Hauser's - Forget-me-not - Eyelet and Scribble Leaf Worksheet

EXAMPLES OF DARK - MEDIUM AND LIGHT FORGET ME NOTS

EYELET

VERY THIN P.B.

WHITE PLUS A TOUCH OF R.B.

WHITE

PAINT FIVE COMMA LIKE STROKES FROM OUTSIDE EDGE OF PETAL "IN" TOWARD THE CENTER

WHITE - TURP

DOUBLE LOAD BRUSH WITH TURP AND WHITE - PAINT EYELET

DIP BRUSH IN TURP - BLOT AND CLEAN OUT HOLES IN EYELET.

B.U.

OUTLINE HOLES ON OUTSIDE EDGE IN THIN WHITE - INSIDE EDGE B.U.

SHADE OUTSIDE EDGE WITH B.U. AND TURP

LINES ARE WHITE

APPLY COLORS - PAINT DARK FLOWERS

PAINT MEDIUM VALUE FLOWERS

PAINT LIGHT VALUE FLOWERS. CENTERS ARE C.Y.L. AND LAMP BLACK

These are so dainty to paint.

THE JAGGED EDGED "SCRIBBLE" LEAF
MEDIUM VALUE

"U" AROUND THE CORNER

C.Y.M.
Y.L.
L.G.M.

BT. UMBER — L.G.M.

DOUBLE LOAD BRUSH WITH L.G.M. AND BT. UMBER AND "SCRIBBLE" THE COLOR ON THE LEAF

SCRIBBLE L.G.M. AND WHITE ON THE OTHER SIDE

ADD COLORS TO EACH SECTION

DARK VALUE
COLORS:
L.G.D.
BT. UMBER
ICE BLUE

LIGHT VALUE
COLORS:
L.G.L.
BT. UMBER
C.Y.L.
WHITE

"LIGHTLY" BLEND FROM THE BASE - OUT INTO EACH SECTION THE VEIN LEAF PULL VEIN IN AN "S" STROKE MANNER

W-3.

C-4.

C-5.

C-6.

C-7.

Priscilla Hauser's Daisy Worksheet

UNDERCOAT IN COLOR OF CHOICE -
I HAVE USED IVORY BLACK.
UNDERCOAT MUST BE THIN
THE CENTER

APPLY PERMALBA WHITE
OVER THE UNDERCOAT.
PAINT MUST BE A
"WHIPPED" CREAM CONSISTANCY

PAINT CENTER
AND DOTS

 8.5. —  C.Y.M.

I UNDERCOATED THE
CENTER IN WHITE - BECAUSE
ITS ON A BLACK BACKGROUND.
I USED WHITE ACRYLIC - LET
DRY

DOTS OF
WHITE - B.U. AND
A FEW C.R.L.
PAINT MUST BE
INK LIKE
CONSISTANCY
DOTS SHOULD BE
"LOOSE."

— LAMP BLACK

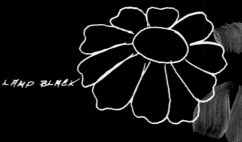

IN A GROUP OF DAISIES
THE BACK DAISIES MUST
BE DARKER THE FRONT
FLOWERS - LIGHTER.

I USED LAMP BLACK
TO UNDERCOAT THE BACK
DAISY - IVORY BLACK ON THE
FRONT DAISY

IVORY
BLACK

UNDERCOAT DAISY CENTERS
IN WHITE ACRYLIC IF DESIRED

H-4.

HAUSER

C-8.

C-9.

C-10.

Priscilla Hauser's Mum Worksheet

C.Y.L.

C.Y.M.

B.S.

APPLY THE DESIRED
COLORS TO THE
"BALL" AND BLEND

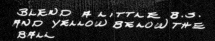

BLEND A LITTLE B.S.
AND YELLOW BELOW THE
BALL

PAINT TWO
COMMA LIKE
STROKES
AT THE TOP OF
THE BALL

STROKES ARE
THIN (WHIPPED
CREAM)
PERMALBA
WHITE.

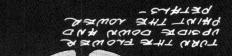

TURN THE FLOWER
UPSIDE DOWN AND
PAINT THE LOWER
PETALS—

FILL-IN WITH MORE
STROKES – DO NOT
WIPE THE BRUSH AND
PICK UP MORE PAINT
UNLESS YOU HAVE TO.
YOU WANT THE
FLOWER TO
SHADE DARKER
AS YOU WORK
TOWARD THE
BOTTOM OF THE
BALL.

A SECOND
ROW OF
PETALS
MAY BE
PAINTED
INBETWEEN
THE FIRST ROW
OF LOWER
PETALS.

HAUSER

W-5.

C-12.   *C-13.*

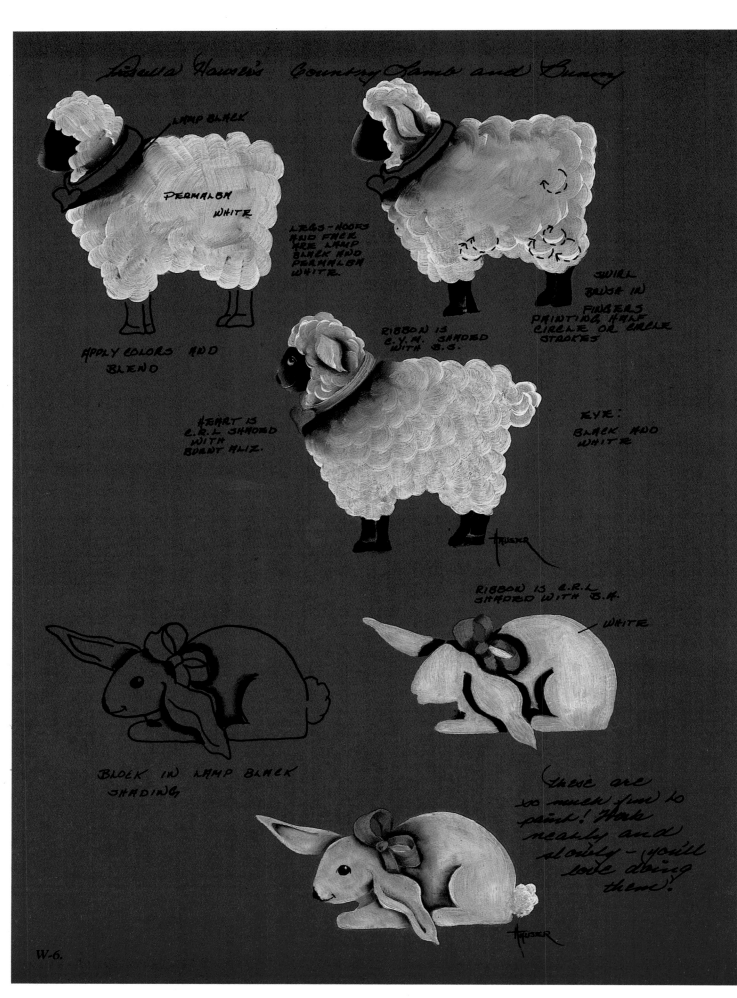

Priscilla Hauser's Country Lamb and Bunny

LAMP BLACK

PERMALON
WHITE

APPLY COLORS AND
BLEND

LEGS-HOOKS
AND FACE
ARE LAMP
BLACK AND
PERMALON
WHITE.

SWIRL
BRUSH IN
FINGERS
PAINTING. HALF
CIRCLE OR CIRCLE
STROKES

RIBBON IS
C.Y.M. SHADED
WITH B.S.

HEART IS
C.R.L. SHADED
WITH
BURNT ALIZ.

EYE:
BLACK AND
WHITE

RIBBON IS C.R.L.
SHADED WITH B.A.

WHITE

BLOCK IN LAMP BLACK
SHADING

These are
so much fun to
paint! Work
neatly and
slowly - you'll
love doing
them!

W-6.

C-14.

C-15.

C-16.

C-17.

C-18.

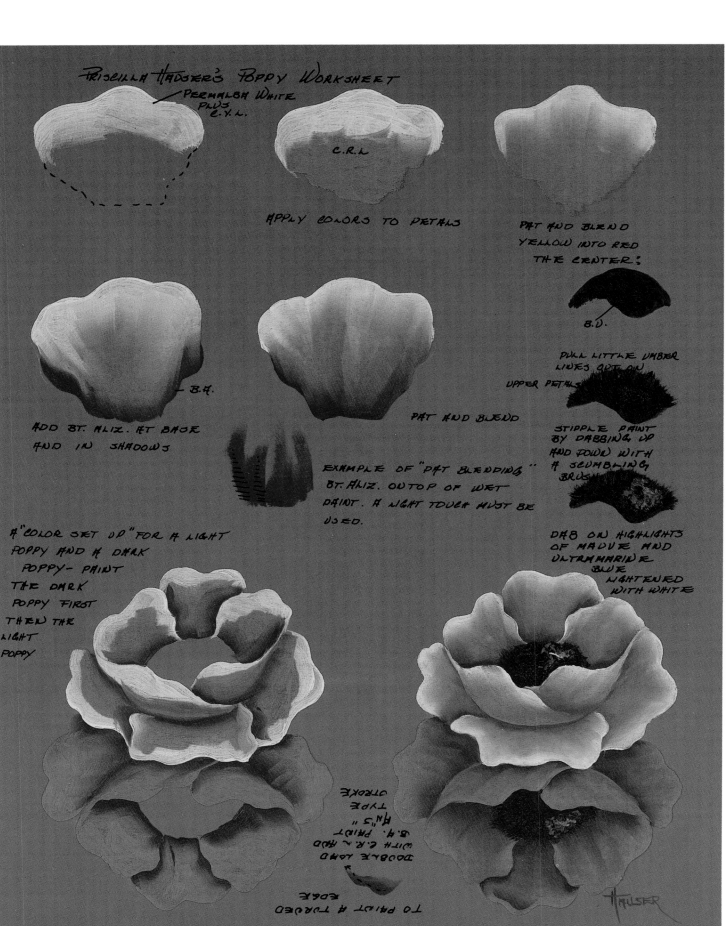

Priscilla Hauser's Poppy Worksheet

Permalba White
Plus
C.Y.L.

APPLY COLORS TO PETALS

PAT AND BLEND
YELLOW INTO RED
THE CENTER:

C.R.L.

B.U.

B.A.

ADD BT. ALIZ. AT BASE
AND IN SHADOWS

PAT AND BLEND

PULL LITTLE UMBER
LINES OUT ON
UPPER PETALS

STIPPLE PAINT
BY DABBING UP
AND DOWN WITH
A SCUMBLING
BRUSH

EXAMPLE OF "PAT BLENDING"
BT. ALIZ. ON TOP OF WET
PAINT. A LIGHT TOUCH MUST BE
USED.

A "COLOR SET UP" FOR A LIGHT
POPPY AND A DARK
POPPY- PAINT
THE DARK
POPPY FIRST
THEN THE
LIGHT
POPPY

DAB ON HIGHLIGHTS
OF MAUVE AND
ULTRAMARINE
BLUE
LIGHTENED
WITH WHITE

TO PAINT A FORCED
EDGE
DOUBLE LOAD
WITH C.R.L. AND
B.A. PAINT
A "S"
TYPE
STROKE

HAUSER

W-7.

C-19.

C-20.

C-21.

Priscilla Hauser's Basic and Advanced Rose Worksheet

APPLY DOT
— BURNT ALIZ.

PAINT UPSIDE DOWN "U" STROKE

PAINT RIGHTSIDE UP "U" STROKE

PAINT QUARTER CIRCLE STROKES AROUND THE BASE.

PAINT 1ST STROKE

DOUBLE LOAD FLAT BRUSH WITH BT. ALIZ. AND PERMALBA WHITE PLUS BT. ALIZ. PAINT MUST BE THIN AND BRUSH FULL!

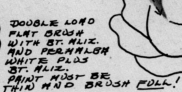
NOW PAINT COMMAS

PAINT A STROKE INBETWEEN THE COMMAS.

MORE LITTLE STROKES

TWO MORE COMMAS

Please practice you'll love painting roses!

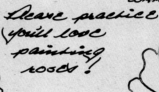
PAINT FIRST BASE OR BOWL PLEASE NOTE WHERE "U" STROKE BEGINS AND ENDS.

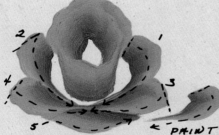
2 1
4 3
5
PAINT FOUR LARGE COMMAS AND ONE "S" STROKE AROUND THE BASE.

PAINT A SECOND BASE OR BOWL ACROSS THE FIRST BOWL THIS IS ALSO A "U" STROKE

"FILL IN" PETALS ARE THIN COMMAS

PAINT MORE THIN "FILL-IN" PETALS

PAINT A ROLLED "S" STROKE TO CONNECT THE TAIL OF ONE COMMA TO THE TAIL OF ANOTHER COMMA.

FILL IN CENTER WITH BT. ALIZ.

W-8.

C-22.

C-23.

C-24.

C-25.

Priscilla Hauser's Strawberry Worksheet

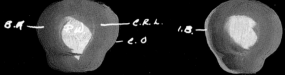

B.A. — P.W. — C.R.L. — C.O.   I.B.

APPLY COLORS

LIGHTLY BLEND
FROM TOP TO BOTTOM
AND BOTTOM TO TOP

CAREFULLY ADD
SEEDS OF C.Y.L.
PAINT MUST BE
THIN. SEEDS
MUST CURVE
WITH SHAPE
OF BERRY.

STRAWBERRY BRACTS

PAINT "U" STROKES
WITH L.G.M. AND B.U.

PAINT AN "S"
STROKE OF B.U.
AND L.G.M.
THEN AN "S" STROKE
OF L.G.M AND WHITE

ADD A
LITTLE Y.C.
TO THE
CENTER
AND BLEND.

AN   UNRIPE   BERRY

ON A BLACK
OR DARK   BACKGROUND
IF DESIRED - UNDERCOAT
BERRY IN WHITE ACRYLIC -
LET DRY -

Y.C. — P.W. — C.R.L — B.A.

APPLY COLORS

BLEND BERRY -
ADD SEEDS - PAINT
BRACTS - NOTICE
SEEDS MAYBE
OUTLINED - IF DESIRED
WITH A FINE HAIRLIKE
LINE OF LAMP BLACK.

COLOR SET UP FOR A DARK
AND LIGHT BERRY

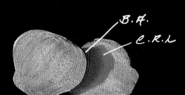

B.A.
C.R.L

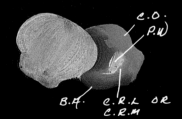

C.O.
P.W
B.A. C.R.L OR
C.R.M

HAUSER

W-9.

11 Poppies

Poppies, poppies, poppies—how gorgeous, how light and airy. They are almost transparent as they blow and move gracefully in the breeze. What a thrill it was for me, when traveling in France, to see the fields of orange poppies. Our own beautiful California produces mountains that glow like fire with poppies. There are many different varieties of poppies, and they are not particularly difficult to paint. They do take more time than the brush-stroke flowers, however, because they are pat blended petal by petal.

The centers of the poppies are breathtaking and very involved. I have simplified the technique for painting the centers. It is effective, but if you desire, the very detailed centers can be painted by studying the actual flower.

Turn to the color section and take a look at the poppies I painted on the trunk (C-19), table leaf (C-20), and school desk (C-21). The patterns for these are figures 13-18, 13-19, and 13-20.

Colors

The colors used on the worksheet (W-7) are: Permalba White, Cadmium Yellow Light, Cadmium Red Light, and Burnt Alizarin.

The colors used for the center are: Burnt Umber, Ultramarine Blue, Permalba White, and Mauve.

Brushes

The size of the brush you use depends upon the size of the poppy you are painting. When you are pat blending, you should always use a brush as large as you can possibly handle, so that there won't be so many tiny, choppy brush strokes showing. On the color worksheet, I used #8, #10, and #12 Priscilla Hauser flat red-sable brushes.

For the center, I used a #4 flat brush and a #4 scumbling or bristle brush.

Painting

Before painting a poppy, study it. Generally, the poppies that I draw will have five to seven petals showing. The petal that is farthest back should be a #1, and it should be painted first. The petals on either side of the back petal would be #2 and #3, and they would be painted next. Continue to paint from the back forward until you have painted all the petals.

It is important to complete one petal at a time. Don't try to apply the color to all the petals at once. It simply won't work, and your painting will be sloppy.

Cream the colors on your palette to a thick, heavy consistency—like spreadable cake icing, but not thin at all.

Please don't laugh at me when I say "You have to understand how a petal moves." If you study my drawings, you will see that I have provided little lines that show you the direction in which each petal flows. If you do not blend in the direction that each petal is flowing, the petal will not look like it is actually a part of the flower. The color in each petal flows outward from the center, following the shape of the petal. Remember, too, that the shape of each petal you paint will be different. Now that you have prepared your paints and studied my drawings, do the following:

1. To Permalba White, add a little Cadmium Yellow Light. Apply this color to the top of the first petal you are painting. Wipe the brush; then pick up some Cadmium Red Light and apply it below the Cadmium Yellow Light mixture. Wipe the brush and place half of the brush on the red and half on the yellow. Gently pat the colors together.

2. Wipe the brush again and lightly pull or pat

the light color down into the red. If you neglect to do this, the red will completely take over the lighter color.

3. Wipe the brush and apply Burnt Alizarin in the shadowed areas. Wipe the brush again and blend, first by stroking, then by patting.

Pat blending requires a very light touch—almost as light as if you were blending and moving the hairs on your arm. It takes practice to develop this type of touch, but it is well worth it.

4. After you have completed the first petal, move on to the second petal, the third petal, and so on, until the flower is complete.

On the color worksheet, I have provided you with step-by-step techniques for painting a light poppy. I have also given you colors for a darker poppy. Paint the darker flowers (i.e., those underneath) first, then the lighter flowers.

Poppy Center. Paint the center of the poppy as follows:

1. Using a #4 brush, neatly and carefully apply Burnt Umber to the entire center.

2. Using a #4 scumbling brush, ever so carefully feather or pull just a touch of Burnt Umber out onto each petal.

3. Now, using your scumbling brush, stipple or rough up the Burnt Umber in the center.

4. To highlight the center, lighten Ultramarine Blue and Mauve with some Permalba White. Dab just a little of each of these colors in the center, as shown on the worksheet.

Poppy Leaves. The poppy leaves are rough with jagged edges. The scribble-leaf technique lends itself beautifully to these leaves. Be sure to use a touch of Burnt Sienna and perhaps a tiny touch of Cadmium Red Light in the base or bottom of the poppy leaves.

12 Roses

My love affair with roses began when I was about twelve years old. I realized how beautiful roses looked, how beautiful they smelled, and how soft they were to touch. Their many different colors continue to fascinate me. Roses say something to everyone. They say "I love you," they say "I'm sorry," they say "thank you." I can't think of another flower that has touched everyone's life in so many ways. You'll love the roses painted on the trunk, music box, pillow, and egg. (See color photographs C-22 through C-25 and the patterns in figures 13-21 through 13-24.)

If you want to learn to paint roses, you must pay your dues. You have to learn the basic brush strokes, you have to learn double loading, and you have to be willing to practice. If you will do these things, you will paint roses and you will paint them beautifully.

First of all, it is important to paint the little basic rose. It takes five steps to create this wonderful little flower. After you have painted 100—yes, that is what I said, 100—of the basic roses, then you can begin to practice the brush strokes that will enable you to create the advanced rose.

Each year in my Victorian "studio by the sea" on the Gulf near Panama City Beach, Florida, I teach a special rose seminar for five students. These people have to love roses in order to come to this seminar, and the results are fabulous. I won't let anyone leave without being able to create this wonderful flower.

You can paint these flowers simply by making a commitment to yourself to practice.

Basic Rose

Colors

For the pink rose, you will need two colors: for one, use Burnt Alizarin; for the other use a mixture of Permalba White to which you have added a touch of Burnt Alizarin. This will make a beautiful light pink.

For the yellow rose, use Cadmium Yellow Light and Burnt Sienna.

Brushes

The size of the brush will depend upon the size of the rose you are painting. On the color worksheet (W-8), I have used a #6 flat red-sable brush for the basic rose.

Painting

To paint these little basic roses, you must follow a set of rules. If you do as directed, however, you will paint them easily:

1. You must have a fine red-sable brush that is in excellent condition.
2. You must thin your paint with odorless turp to a very loose, bird-blessing consistency.
3. You must practice the basic brush strokes with the flat brush.
4. You must know and understand excellent double-loading techniques.

Study the color worksheet (W-8) in great detail. Lay a sheet of tracing paper or clear acetate on top of my worksheet; dry-brush practice the strokes on top of mine. Then fill your brush and try painting them many, many times.

Now you are ready to begin painting the roses:

1. Apply a dot of Burnt Alizarin in the center of the rose.
2. Double load the flat brush with the Burnt Alizarin and the pink mixture. Blend on the palette to soften the color; go back and fill the brush completely again.

Paint an upside-down "U" around the dot of color, as shown on the color worksheet, touching the color with the corner of the brush and blending the color up into the petal.

3. To paint the base or bowl of the rose, stand the brush on the flat edge, let it join the corner of the upper stroke, pull down, and paint a "U" stroke.

4. If necessary, pick up a little of the pink mixture and fill in underneath the center. Wipe the brush and completely restroke the base of the rose.

5. Now add the five little petals around the base or bowl. These petals are approximately a quarter of a circle—not a half of a circle—in size. It is usually easier if you turn the flower upside down and stroke from left to right. (A left-handed person, of course, will need to reverse what I am doing.) If it is easier for you to paint a quarter circle on the right side and one on the left side, feel free to do it that way.

You may go back over any of the strokes, but don't pick at them. Each stroke must be complete. It is easy to make a mistake—that is why it is necessary to practice so much. Don't be discouraged when you make a mistake; just clean your brush, double load, and start over again.

Advanced Rose

I ask you not to try the advanced rose until you have painted at least 100 of the basic roses. The reason for this is that I don't want you to become frustrated. Painting advanced roses is not at all difficult *if* you have paid your dues and you are ready for them.

Colors

Use the same colors that are used for the Basic Rose.

Brushes

On the color worksheet, I have used a #10 flat red-sable brush in excellent condition.

Painting

1. Double load the brush with the light pink mixture on one side and the Burnt Alizarin on the other. Blend on the palette to soften the color. Be sure that your brush is completely full of paint and that the paint has the proper consistency. (It should flow freely from the hairs of the brush.)

2. Paint the center stroke of the back row of petals. The light pink is always to the outside when painting the petals. This stroke is a scalloped stroke.

3. Paint a scalloped commalike stroke to the right of the center stroke. This stroke must lift to a beautiful flat edge as you come toward the center of the rose.

4. Paint the same type of stroke on the left side of the rose.

5. Check the strokes that you have painted to be sure that the Burnt Alizarin color is good and strong. If it is not, now is the time to go back over each stroke carefully and strengthen the color.

6. The second row of petals is painted on top of the back row. When the second row is painted, the light pink edge must show against the dark pink in the first row of petals. You can see this on the color worksheet. The strokes in the second row are much lighter than the strokes in the first row. The brush is still double loaded with the light pink mixture and the Burnt Alizarin, as it is throughout the painting of the rose. Keep your strokes high.

7. To paint the first base or bowl of the rose, stand the brush on the flat edge. Attach the tail of the comma on the inside or second row of petals to the edge of the bowl. Study this step on the color worksheet. Slide down, press, and lift up, joining the tail of the comma on the other side. This is a "U" stroke that cuts across the front of the flower forming the base or bowl.

8. Now paint the outside petals. Place the double-loaded brush so that the stroke appears to come from behind the upper row of petals. You will see this done on the worksheet. The outside petals are scalloped comma strokes. There are two of these scalloped comma strokes on each side, for a total of four strokes. The fifth stroke, which is painted across the bottom, is an "S" stroke. Once again, go to the worksheet and find the five outside petals, four commas, and the "S" stroke at the bottom.

9. Paint a second base or bowl across the front of the rose. Stand the brush on the flat edge on the left-hand side and let it join the tail of the back comma.

Again, pull down and paint a "U" stroke over the front of the rose. This goes on top of the first base or bowl you painted but drops down slightly lower.

10. The fill-in petals are painted on top of the outside petals. Be sure that you have good strong color on the outside petals so that when you paint the fill-in comma strokes on top, they will show up. The paint must be very thin. The strokes themselves are slender comma strokes. There is no precise number of fill-in petal strokes. I use as many as seem to be needed on each rose, and each rose turns out a little bit different. Study the fill-in strokes on the worksheet.

11. "Rolling" a petal across the base of the rose is not a difficult thing to do. The stroke is actually a rolled "S", and its function is to connect the tail or edge of one fill-in petal to the tail or edge of another. In doing so, a petal is formed that cups over the base or bowl of the rose. Study the rolled petal on the color worksheet; then study your practice rose. Find the tail of a comma on one side that you want to connect to a tail on the other side. Then stand the brush on its flat edge, pull, let the brush roll forward, and continue to drag and connect to the tail on the other side.

12. At this point, once again, study your rose to see if the edges of any more petals need to be painted. I call these edges slices, and they take some practice to do. The sliced-in edges should look like the edges of a rose petal that is just starting to roll back. Sometimes you may paint a rose that turns out so nicely that slices or little fill-in petals aren't needed.

13. The final step is to complete the center of the rose. Double load your flat brush with the Burnt Alizarin on one side and the light pink on the other side. Blend on the palette to soften the color. With the light pink on top, scallop a third row of petals into the upper portion of the rose center. Some of these strokes should be high and some should drop down a little lower on each side. Keep the throat or the center very dark with the Burnt Alizarin.

All of this sounds far more complicated than it really is. I wish you could see me do this—and if you ever have the opportunity, call your Public Television Station and ask for Priscilla Hauser's "Magic of Decorative Painting." To watch me paint a rose would be worth a million words. However, many, many people have learned to paint them simply from the instructions in my book and the self-discipline it takes to learn. All of us have been given the ability to learn. Oh please, just take the time to do it.

13 Patterns

Some of the patterns have been reduced to fit on the book page. The simplest way to enlarge them to full size is to take them to a copy center. The caption will tell you by how much the pattern has been reduced.

13-1. Pattern for folk art dining chair.

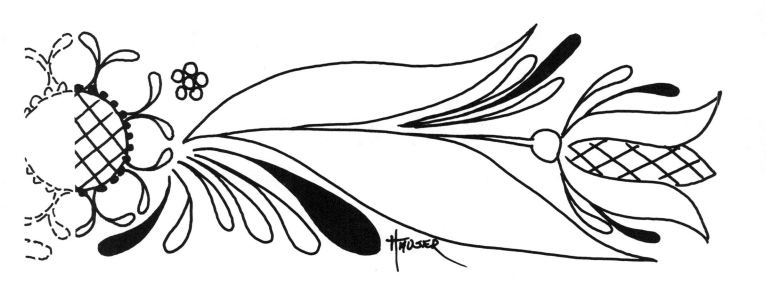

13-2a. Pattern for folk art tavern sign.

~All ye who enter~
must wear a
Smile

13-2b. Pattern for folk art tavern sign.

13-2c. Pattern for folk art tavern sign.

13-3. Pattern for folk art wine rack.

13-4. Pattern for forget-me-nots pencil box.

13-5. Pattern for forget-me-nots vanity mirror.

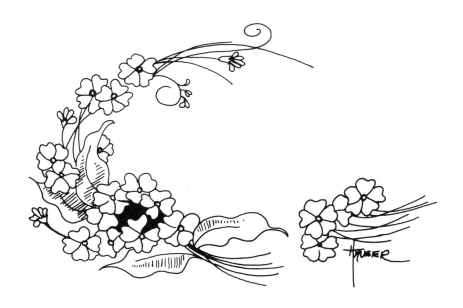

13-6. Pattern for forget-me-nots potpourri box.

13-7. Pattern for forget-me-nots piano music box.

13-8a. Pattern for strawberries dining chair.

13-8b. Pattern for strawberries dining chair.

(Top of old chair back)

13-9a. Pattern for strawberries crate.

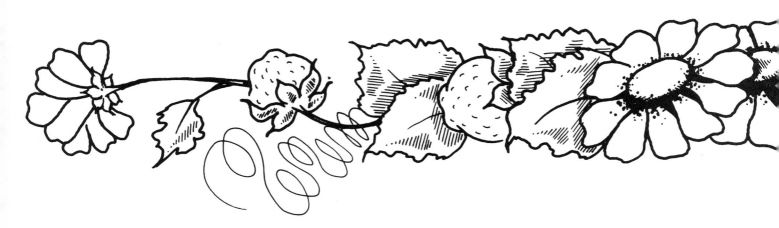

13-9b. Pattern for strawberries crate.

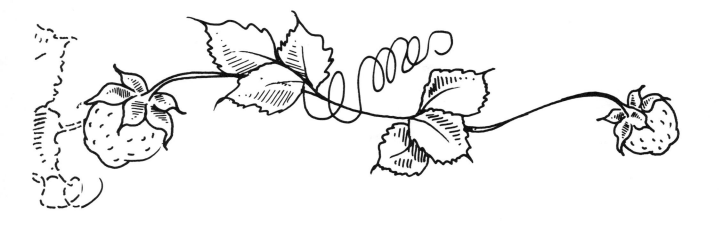

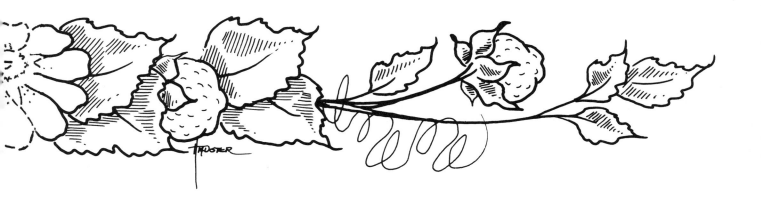

13-10. Pattern for strawberries clock.

this is wonderful
on the face of a
clock -- but --
lends itself to
many other projects.

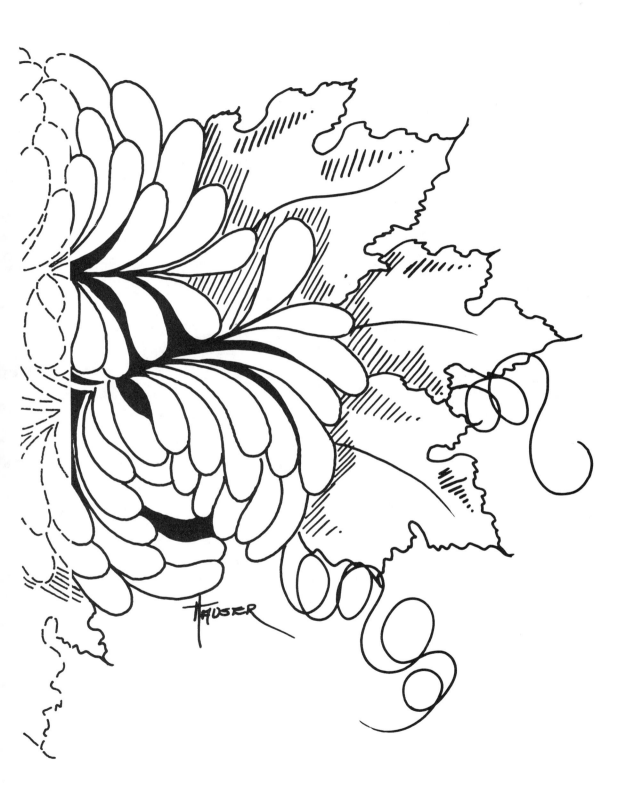

13-11. Pattern for mums and daisies footstool.

13-12. Pattern for mums and daisies music box.

This Mum design
was used on the
oval Music Box.
Notice that it
can be viewed
correctly from
any angle.

13-13a. Pattern for mums and daisies trunk (right side).

13-13b. Pattern for mums and daisies trunk (left side).

13-13c. Pattern for mums and daisies trunk (trunk top) reduced by 20 percent.

13-13d. Pattern for mums and daisies trunk (top pattern) reduced by 10 percent.

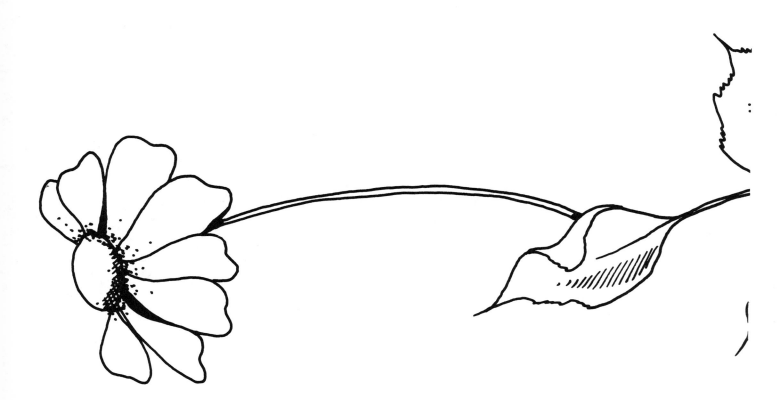

13-14. Pattern for bunny trunk reduced by 5 percent.

13-15. Pattern for bunny plaque.

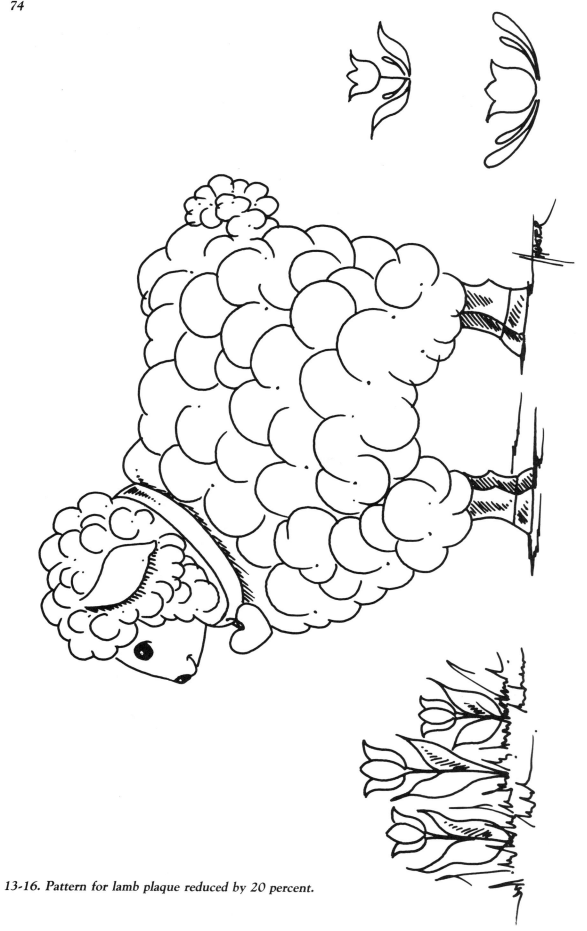

13-16. Pattern for lamb plaque reduced by 20 percent.

13-17. Pattern for lamb wreath and picnic basket.

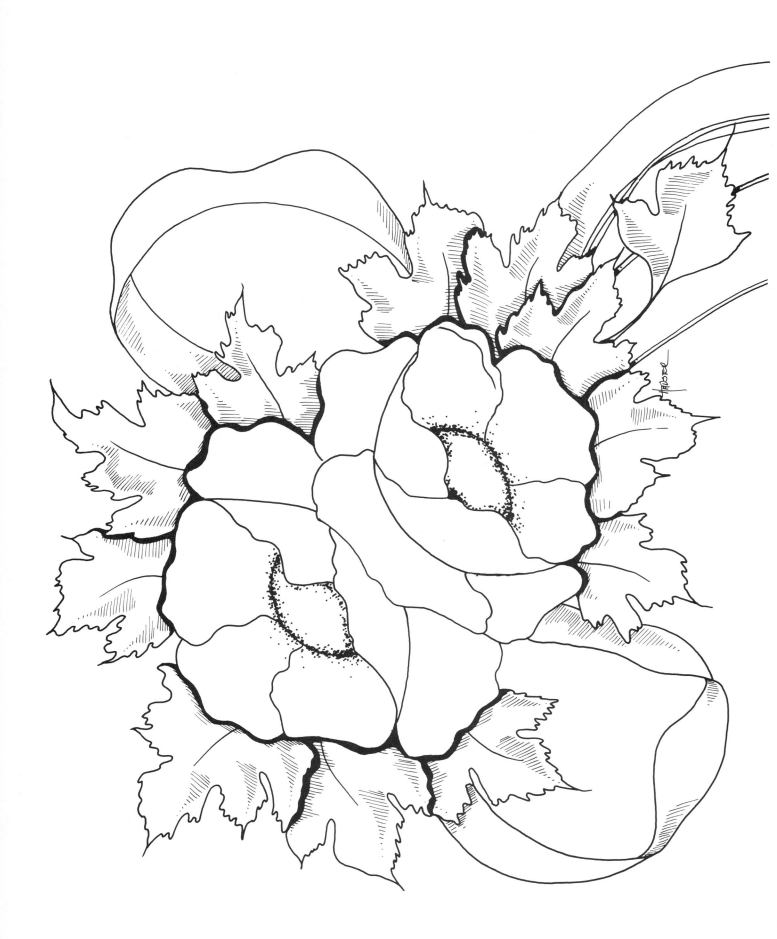

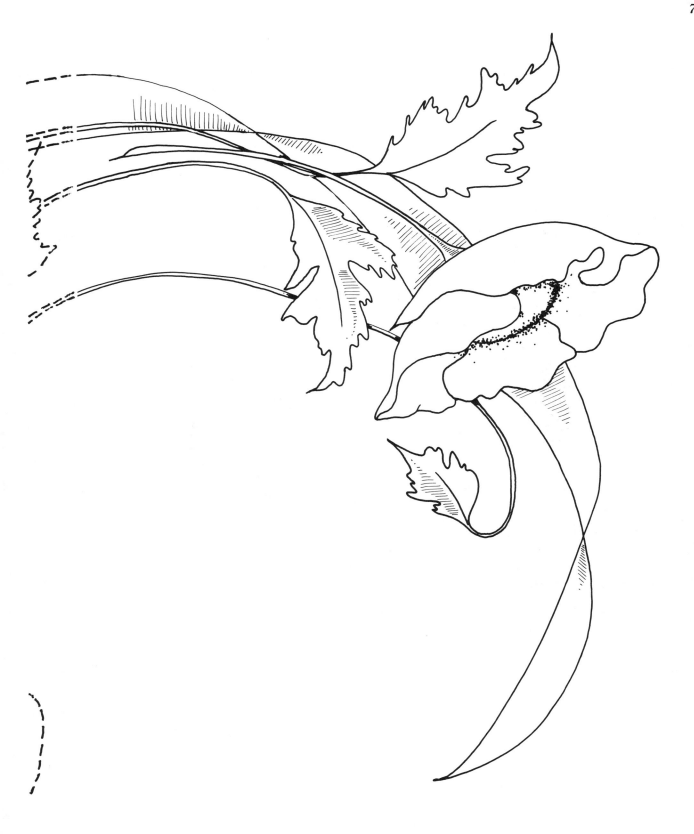

13-18. Pattern for poppies trunk reduced by 40 percent.

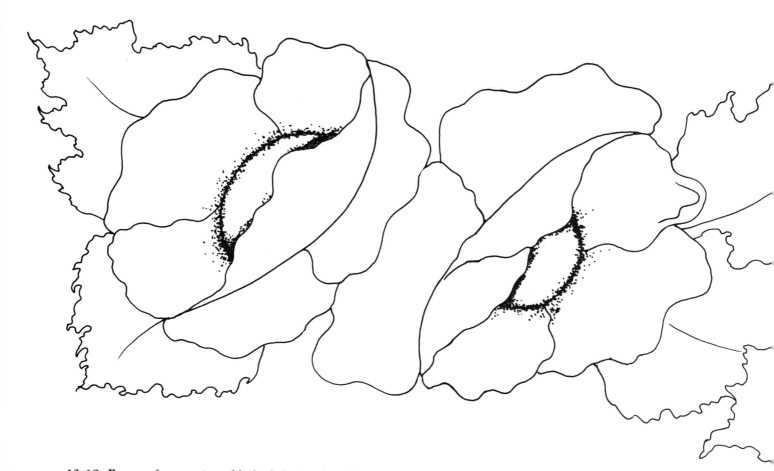

13-19. Pattern for poppies table leaf (leg) reduced by 55 percent.

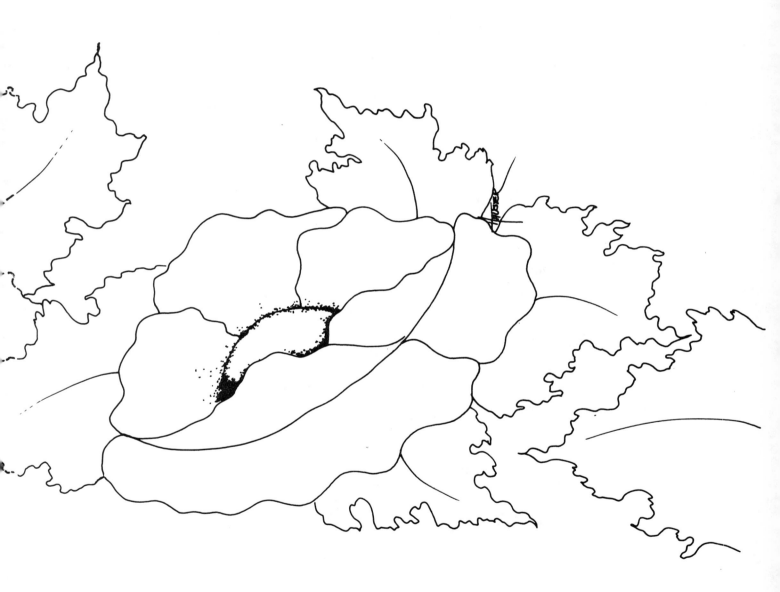

13-20a. *Pattern for poppies school desk (seat).*

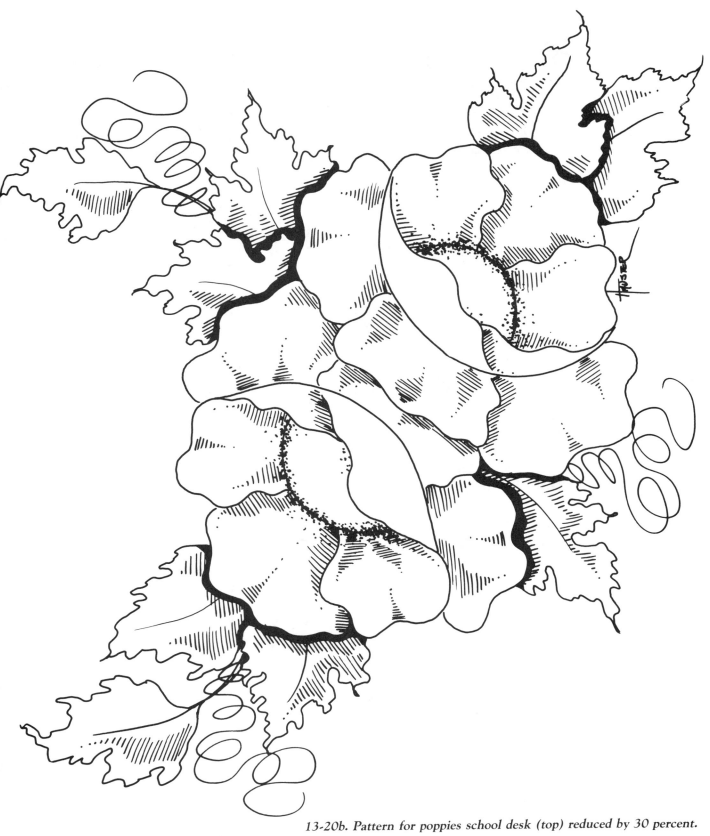

13-20b. Pattern for poppies school desk (top) reduced by 30 percent.

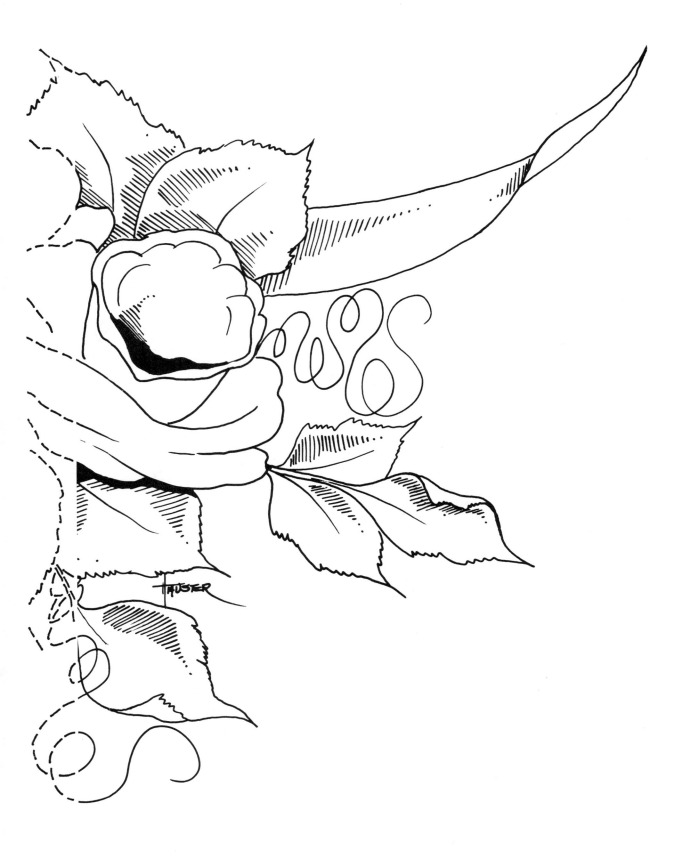

13-21a. Pattern for roses camelback trunk (top) reduced by 20 percent.

13-21b. Pattern for roses camelback trunk (top pattern).

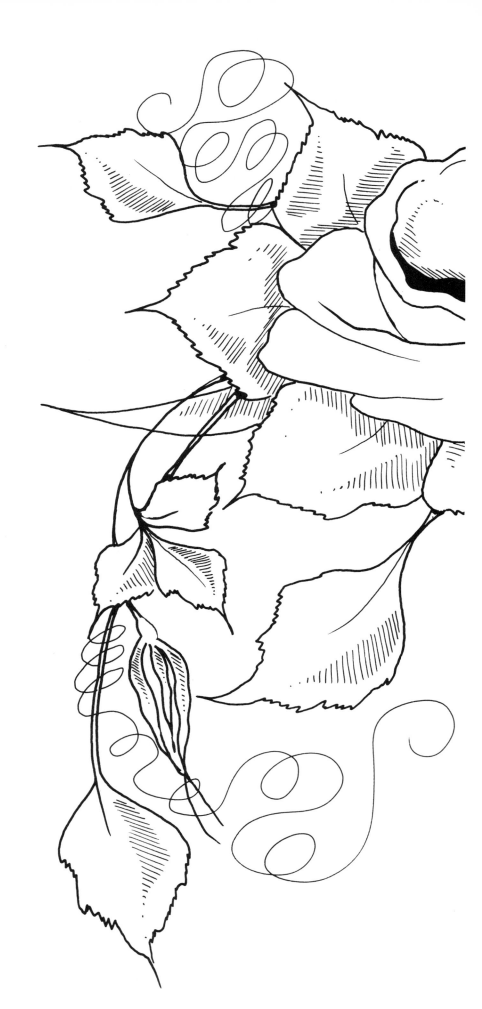

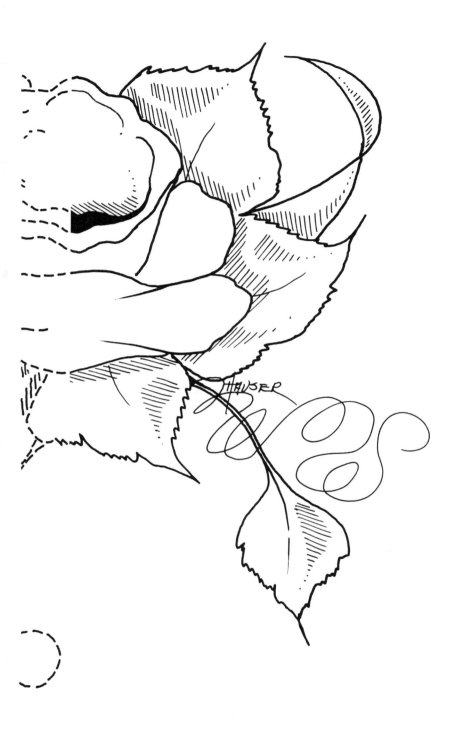

13-21c. Pattern for roses camelback trunk (end pattern).

13-22. Pattern for heart music box.

13-23. Pattern for roses pillow.

13-24. Pattern for roses egg.

Priscilla at her studio by the sea.

Sources

The supplies mentioned in this book are readily available at local art- and craft-supply stores. If you have trouble finding any of them, the following are reliable mail-order sources. Write for a catalog to:

Priscilla's Little Red Tole House
P.O. Box 521013
Tulsa, OK 74152-1013

Rural Rustics
2250 Old Nadea Road
Palmdale, CA 93550

Folk Art by Judy
163 Siegel Blvd.
Babylon, NY 11702

The Tole Box
Rte. 1
Box 312
Colfax, WI 54730

Priscilla Hauser Accredited Teachers

Alabama

Genie Amberson, 3525 Mill Run Rd., Birmingham 35223

Jolene Anderson, 318 Coffee Ave. N.E., Russellville 35653

Ceil Bates, P.O. Box 503, Millbrook 36054

Jean Beckstrom, Rte. 1, Box 134A, Equality 36026

Jackie Burt, 505 Vincent Rd., S.E., Huntsville 35804

Carolyn Camp, Rte. 4, Box 251K, Athens 35611

Jane Carroll, 502 Mayo, Dothan 36301

Carolyn Collier, Athens Plaza, Athens 35611

Tricia Dempsey, 2500 Willena Dr., Huntsville 35803

Jan Dukes, 1002 Oakbowery Rd., Opelika 36801

Bob Embry, Northside Mall, Ross Clark Circle N.W., Dothan 36301

Debra Franklin, 1808 Opelika Road, Phenix City 36867

Jo S. Glenn, 317 Gunter Ave., Wetumpka 36092

Ponselle Haynes, Rte. 1, Box 224, River View 36872

Robert Hays, 3022 Pumphouse Circle, Birmingham 35243

Jackie Heupel, 4155 Strathmore Dr., Montgomery 36116

Lynn Johnson, 430 Palisade, Florence 35630

Helen Johnston, 202 Wind Creek Way, Enterprise 36330

Ryan Kay, 3631 Rainbow Dr., Tuscaloosa 35401

Audrey Kenopke, 8351 Grand Oaks Dr., Theodore 36582

Herbie King, 505 Ardmore Lane, Birmingham 35210

Mary Ann Lemmond, 601 Main St., Hartselle 35640

Mary Louise Radder, 2509 Robin Hood Dr., Mobile 36605

Mae Rainer, 410 Randwick Rd., Dothan 36301

Gerry Rowe, 3335B Old Montgomery Hwy., Birmingham 35209

Grace Schwan, 5408 Cross Creek Dr., Mobile 36609

Mary Ann Scott, 1407 Scott St., Opelika 36801

Doris Shaw, 3819 Malabar Rd., Montgomery 36116

Nancy Simpson, 1029 Antietam Rd. S.E., Huntsville 35803

Kathy Waites, 4321 Millwood Lane, Millbrook 36054

Joann Walker, 314 Hillcrest Ct., Opelika 36801

Hazel Ward, Star Rte., Double Springs 35553

Latrelle Wartman, Rte. 1, Box 292, Ashford 36312

Mary A. Weeks, P.O. Box 305, Hamilton 35570

Dena E. Weygant, P.O. Box 269, Foley 36536

Linda Young, Rte. 5, Box 155, Bob Jones Ave., Scottsboro 35768

Alaska

Virginia Smith, 1020 G St., Anchorage 99503

Arizona

Joyce Barnette, 11601 N. 66th St., Scottsdale 85254

Kathryn Bortel, Towerpoint Resort, Box A44, 4860 E. Mail, Mesa 85205

Penny Cantley, 8743 E. San Miguel, Scottsdale 85252

Mickey Castillo, 514 Morris, Mesa 85201

Emma Celeskey, 2855 N. Lane, Phoenix 85028

Debra Lee Dupray, 12040 Jefsumark Circle, Tucson 85749

Audrey Farrell, 445 N. 96th Pl., Mesa 85207

Ellen French, Rte. 1, Box 167, Somerton 85350

Marti Harnisch, 1167 E. Commonwealth, Chandler 85224

Rita Karis, 4301 N. 63rd Dr., Phoenix 85033

Letia H. Kerlee, 732 S. Penrose Circle, Mesa 85206

Virginia Littlefield, 6730 Calle Padre, Tucson 85701

Ann Litzler, 67 Pine Ridge Dr., Flagstaff 86001

Diane Ponitch, 7402 E. Cortez, Scottsdale 85260

Dorothy Schafer, 8752 E. Hubbel, Scottsdale 85727

Naoma Tyner, 66 Pine Ridge Dr., Flagstaff 86001

Arkansas

Pat Carter, Rte. 4, Kingsberry Estates, Mountain Home 72653

Betty Coger, Rte. 6, Huntsville 72740

Lynnette Collums, Rte. 1, Bee Branch 72013

Peggy Dukat, 825 Hall St., Mountain Home 72653

Margaret Fleming, 2324 E. Matthews, Jonesboro 72401

Gwen Flemister, 1532 Crestwood, N. Little Rock 72116

Margurite Foster, 4200 Idlewild Ave., N. Little Rock 72116

Robin Hawkins, Rte. 8, Box 367, Mountain Lake 72653

Ruth Johnson, 706 Pecan, Crosset 71635

Carol King, 1418 E. Twin Lakes Dr., Little Rock 72205

Brenda Lincoln, 610 Fernwood, Benton 72015

Mollie B. Phillips, 1816 Independence, Conway 73032

Betty Rothwell, R.R. 3, Quitman 72131

Shirley Vaughan, Box 371, Morrilton 72110

California

Dorothy Abrams, 207 E. Fester, Santa Maria 93454

Leslie Ann Adams, 532 Judson Avenue, San Francisco 94112

Vee Adler, 260 Main, Weed 96094

W. Ablene Aimo, 8347 E. Granite Dr., Roseville 95678

B.D. Anderson, 5394 Northway Rd., Pleasanton 94566

Catherine H. Anderson, 1779 Tangle Wood Dr., San Luis Obispo 93401

Frances Anderson, 8600 Links Rd., Buena Park 90621

Margaret Armouchel, 24159 Meadow Falls Dr., Diamond Bar 91765

Karen J. Arney, 1855 N. Marlowe St., Thousand Oaks 91360

Beth Atchison, 4297 Ridge Dr., Pittsburg 94565

Lucille H. Backman, 10670 New Avenue, Gilrey 95020

Donna Bailey, 340 Mesa Rd., Salinas 93908

Llwellyn Baker, 19580 Penzance St., Salinas 93901

Toni Baley, 2208 Gorman, Camarillo 93010

Marianne R. Baptist, 3682 Seven Hills Rd., Castro Valley 94546

Sandra Barrett, 1926 Harbor Blvd., Costa Mesa 92626

Beverly Batdorf, 84 Westbury St., Thousand Oaks 91360

Barbara Battles, 355 Wildflower, Ridgecrest 93555

Ann Beck, 218 Oleander, Bakersfield 93304

Barbara Benett, P.O. Box 745, Main St., Diamond Springs 95619

Patti Bergin, 1171 Nimitz Lane, Foster City 94404

Arlete L. Bishop, 5365 Silver Reef Dr., Fremont 94538

Lernie Black, 3851 Lenden, Long Beach 90807

Doris Bondreau, 1561 Mesa Dr. #3, Santa Ana 92701

Jill Bondy, 23647 Via Calma, Valencia 91355

Kathryn Bonfiglio, 2891 Benjamin Ave., San Jose 95124

Constance F. Boschetto, 8606 7th St., Downey 90241

Joyce Brandfas, 1466 W. Dolphin, Ridgecrest 93555

Pat Bridwell, 4175 Stevens Creed Blvd., Santa Clara 95050

Jean Brown, 369 Birchwood St., Modesto 95350

Lois E. Brown, 72 Contento Ct., San Luis Obispo 93901

Lynnea Brown, 8938 10th Ave., Hesperia 92345

Dorothy Bunting, 40976 Pataro Dr., Fremont 94538

Diane B. Burtsfield, 130 Melrose Ct., Vacaville 95688

Kay Butcher, 1663 Tierra Montanosa, Alpine 92001

Judi Caplan, 5030 Glenwood Ct., Pleasanton 94566

Gladys N. Capps, 229 Stanley Rd., Burlingame 94010

Bernice Caprino, 1564 Willowgate Dr., San Jose 95118

Caroline Caputo, 3318 W. Ave., L-4, Lancaster 93534

Terry Cardoza, 35525 Galen Pl., Fremont 94536

Doris Carlson, 430 Raspberry Pl., Oxnard 93030

Marlene Carr, 2388 Creekwood Ct., Santa Rosa 95405

Karen Castillo, 2129 McCrea Rd., Thousand Oaks 91360

Joanne Cenicola, 7032 Via Serena, San Jose 95139

Etta F. Chinn, 190 Kimberlin Heights Dr., Oakland 94919

Sharon Christensen, 6075 Fremont Circle, Camarillo 93010

Ardis Christman, 2221 Briarfield, Camarillo 93010

Sally Ciphers, P.O. Box 2206, Arnold 95223

Dorothy Cochrane, 9031 9th Ave., Hesperia 92345

Carlene Collins, 6806 Cherrywood, Bakersfield 93308

Phyllis Connolly, P.O. Box 515, Rocklin 95677

Rena Louise Costa, 21601 E. Copperopolis Rd., Linden 95214

Alice Coughlin, 2847 Wentworth Rd., Shingle Springs 95862

Opal Crabtrey, 12801 Newhope, Garden Grove 92043

Marolyn Currier, P.O. Box 214, Smartville 95977

Joan M. Dahl, 1563 Copenhagen Dr., Solvang 93463

Carolyn Danser, 11025 Spruce Ave., Bloomington 92316

Lela Davison, 43 Bellevue Ave., Nada 94558

Alice Deetz, Rte. 1, Box 565, Mt. Shasta 96067

Mary Margaret Dehart, 7 Irving, Victorville 93293

Mary Dennison, 225 Oregon Trail, Palm Springs 92262

Terry De Shields, P.O. Box 73, Trona 93726

Sandra J. Dickinson, 120 El Bonito Way, Millbrae 93304

Lynn H. Dirga, 207 Race St., Grass Valley 95945

Karen Dobbins, 620 Eaton, Dinuba 93618

Darlene Dolan, 1108 Granito Dr., Ojai 93023

Bernice Dolman, 143 San Carlos Ct., Vacaville 95688

Diana Domenghini, 2001 San Bernardo Park Rd., Morro Bay 93442

Elizabeth Doran, 5712 Judith St., San Jose 95123

Dorothy Dow, 719 Valle Vista, Vallejo 94590

Florence Duddridge, 800 Ann Arbor, Bakersfield 93308

Margaret Dumouchel, 24159 Meadow Falls Dr., Diamond Bar 91765

Lillian R. Eckerman, 2977 Flora St., San Luis Obispo 93401

Wendy Fanning, 730 W. San Ramon, Fresno 93704

Marion Foster, 88 Rutherford Lane, Martinez 94553

Jean Fowler, 1224 Solano Ave., Vallejo 94590

Peggy Fowler, 727 Bear Valley, Escondido 92055

Denise Garcia, 3022 Barlow Dr., Castro Valley 94546

Lodema Gartman, 4504 N. Ventura Ave., Ventura 93001

Evelyn P. Geataro, 190 Willow Dr., Solvang 93463

Dorothy Gellert, 2254 Taraval St., San Francisco 94101

Elizabeth Genhardi, P.O. Box 4673, Santa Barbara 93015

Dianne George, 1986 Winston Dr., Fairfield 94533

Selma George, 311 West Center St., Yreka 96097

Norma Gibbs, 24404 Gilmore St., Canoga Park 91307

Martha Gill, 4324 Lagunard, Oxnard 93030

Sandra Gillespie, Rte. 3, Box 192H, San Luis Obispo 93401

Lee Gomez, 16308 Mateo, San Leandro 94578

Laura Lynn Graham, 3567 Stallion Dr., Santa Rosa 95404

Patricia Gray, 127 Inyo Lane, Camp Pendleton 92055

Martha Griffen, 2836 Elvyre Way, Sacramento 95821

Ronda Griswold, 4511 S. Hamilton Ave., Oxnard 93030

Marsha Grove, 1129 W. Young St., Wilmington 90744

Doreen Gwinner, 10324 Richwood Dr., Cupertino 95014

Diana L. Hackett, P.O. Box 7379, Tahoe City 95730

Mary Hogarth, 8605 Seventh St., Downey 90241

Rebecca Haley, P.O. Box 297, Penryn 95663

Carol Hallenbeck, 2625 E. North Bear Creek Dr., Merced 95340

Winona Hanson, 2270 Wisconsin Ave., Redding 96001

Gwen Hare, 2000-15 Ashe Rd., Bakersfield 93309

Doris Harris, 9786 Hawley Rd., El Cajon 92021

Tracy Harrison, 14591 Bowling Green, Westminster 92683

Fran Havens, 38265 Delacour Dr., Palmdale 93550

Joan Heacock, 112 Browns Valley Rd., Watsonville 95076

Mary A. Heller, 2 Monte Veda Dr., Orinda 94536

Sheila Hester, 38645 Landon Ave., Palmdale 93550

Helen Hickish, 2250 Old Nadeau Rd., Palmdale 93550

Patricia Hillman, 51 Del Sol Ct., San Luis Obispo 93401

Patricia Hood, 2523 Dennis Dr., Daly City 94015

Sandy Howell, 816 Marian St., Vallejo 94590

Dorothy Ishimatsu, 5167 Country Lane, San Jose 95129

Phyllis Jacklich, 16053 Via Walter, San Lorenzo 94580

Ruth M. Jacobs, 6542 Fair Ave., North Hollywood 91604

Lenore Jacobson, 111 S. El Monte Ave., Los Altos 94022

Evelyn James, 291 Bayview Ave., Ventura 93003

Jo Sonja Jansen, P.O. Box 9080, Eureka 95501

Barbara Johnson, 176 Kentucky Ave., San Luis Obispo 93401

Ethel Johnson, 29 Littleway Lane, Watsonville 95073

H. Haden Jordan, 168 Virginia St., Haywood 94554

Margo L. Kelly, 53 B. St., Vallejo 94590

Norma Kelly, 1511 Mt. Diablo Ave., Milpitas 95035

Ruth Kelsey, 3690 Olive, Santa Ynez 93460

Carol Kimmel, 442 Marigold Dr., Fairfield 94533

Estelle Kirby, 908 Rosewood Ave., Camarillo 93010

Jean Kistner, 5392 Hilltop Crestaut, Oakland 94618

Alma Knecht, 19939 N. Kennefick Rd., Acampo 95220

Ingrid Knudson, 4137 Bouton Dr., Lakewood 90712

Ora Knudson, 4137 Bouton Dr., Lakewood 90712

Karman Koontz, 2990 Sara Ct., Newbury Park 91320

Barbara Kraft, 1934 Arbor Ave., Belmont 94002

Ella Kulczewski, P.O. Box 131, Monte Rio 94014

Joan Landis, 1382 Gravenstein Hwy. S., Sebastopol 95472

Ruth Lasich, 6720 Elwood Rd., San Jose 95120

Nancy A. Lavender, 10650 Atwood Dr., Rancho Cordova 95670

Wanda Lear, 97 "A" St., Concord 94520

Pauline LePage, 12604 LePage Ranch Rd., Pearblossom 93553

Suzanne Cholet Lewis, 3913 Claremont Dr., Bakersfield 93306

Betty Lindsay, 1918 Arroyo Ave., Oceanside 92054

Carol Lowry, 2501 Banbury Rd., Cambria 93428

Mickey Lynch, 2921 Sherwood Dr., San Carlos 94070

Evelyn MacHue, 4508 Northampton Dr., Carmichael 95608

Micki Martin, 1359 Coventry Ave., Ventura 93003

Rosemarie Martin, 23926 Van Owen, Canoga Park 91304

Virginia Mau, 3524 E. Ave., Rte. 34, Palmdale 93550

Tottie L. McCullough, 1049 E. El Camino Rd., Sunnyvale 94087

Louise McKenna, 2 Kimmie Ct., Belmont 94002

Kathy Meeker, P.O. Box 6066, Suite 208, Santa Maria 93456

Virginia Taft Meeks, 3489 Thunderbird Dr., Concord 94520

Louann Mefford, 8127 Imperial Hwy., Downey 90242

Mary Ellen Merrmer, 3158 St. Martin Way, Sebastopol 95472

Lynn Minor, 1201 E. Fairhaven, Santa Ana 92701

Bee Mitchell, 911 Dianna Dr., Lodi 95240

Lila Molner, 163 San Benito, Ventura 93004

Thais Moore, 5712 Twin Oaks Rd., Mariposa 95338

Lois Morrow, 1052 Bella Dr., Napa 94558

Margaret Munsey, 1554 Audre Dr., Anaheim 92802

Don Namestka, 3664 Agnes Ave., Lynwood 90262

Shelly Nealon, 1380 Piland Dr., San Jose 95130

Barbara Neilsen, 1259 Bedford St., Fremont 94538

Varsha Nelson, 18821 Donington St., Glendora 91740

Connie Nolan, 2151 Oakland Rd., Space 141, San Jose 95131

Lenna North, 3389 Walker Mine Rd., Redding 96001

Yukie O'Hara, 932 September Dr., Cupertino 95014

Geri O'Malley, 406 Balsam Ave., Bakersfield 93305

Joyce Ortner, 5379 Santa Rosa Lane, Carpenteria 93013

Kristen Osgood, 1530 Pamela Crest, Redlands 92373

Marilyn Osgood, 179 Canon Dr., Santa Barbara 93105

Margie Ostrander, 3540 Matilija Canyon Rd., Ojai 93023

Ann C. Otis, 8993 San Luis, South Gate 90280

Beverly Owens, 3161 Boeing Rd., Cameron Park 95682

Rusty Parle, 6108 Heather Lane, Kelseyville 95451

Linda Parlet, 83470 Amargosa Ave., Trona 93562

Pat Peguesse, 2550 E. Ave. I. No. III, Lancaster 93534

Bobbie Lee Pellerin, 6146 Etiwanda, Mira Loma 91752

Cherlene Ann Post, 1410 Ridley Ave., Hacienda Heights 91745

Irene Prigger, 2310 Kingsbridge Lane, Oxnard 93030

Marlene Quitney, 1510 Hillcrest Rd., Hollister 94023

Betti Raaf, 6500 Mt. Whitney Dr., Bakersfield 93309

Marla Radcliffe, 9826 Flamingo, Fountain Valley 92708

Mildred Rawson, 38470 N. Tenth Pl. E., Palmdale 93550

Della Renshaw, 605A E. Oak St., Ojai 93023

Ferre Rhinehart, 1651 Canby Rd., Redding 96002

Mary Ribet, 5664 Calle Real, Golita 93017

Pat Riggs, 10902 Cochran, Riverside 92505

Barbara Roberts, 637 Eadington Ave., Fullerton 92634

Virginia Robertson, 3025 W. Beverly Blvd., Montebello 90640

Nancy Rodgers, 1741 Chelsea Rd., Palos Verdes Estates 90274

Roberta Rothel, 1382 Gravenstein Hwy. S., Sebastopol 95472

Doris Scarborough, P.O. Box 751, Lawndale 90260

Pat Schmidt, 6824 Somerville Way, Fair Oaks 95628

Avis Schneider, 4151 E. Holland, Fresno 93726

Gloria Schneider, P.O. Box 568, Lower Lake 95457

Vi Schuttler, R.R. #1, Box 102A, Willow Creek Rd., Paso Nobles 93346

Florence G. Seward, 4201 Montair St., Long Beach 90808

Claire Shea, 3258 Overland Ave., Los Angeles 90034

Clete Sherman, 252 E. Fender Ave. N., Fullerton 92631

Jessie Shoffield, 18297 Jacaranda, Fountain Valley 92908

Virginia Sileski, 6331 Athena Dr., Huntington Beach 92647

Didna Silva, P.O. Box K., Sunol 94586

Frances E. Silva, Rte. 4, Box 4558, Orland 95963

Gerry L. Silva, Star Rte. 1, Box 300, Etna 96027

Alice E. Skoog, 168 University Ave., Ventura 93003

Pat Slagle, 740 Park Dr., Bakersfield 93306

Michele Smith, 427 Blaine Ave., Fillmore 93015

Linda Smithson, 455 Berkshire Dr., Dixon 95620

Loeta F. Sorenson, 225 Lometa Ave., No. 11, Sunnyvale 92708

Toni Speth, 17601 Locust, Fountain Valley 92708

Tami Spirito, 9 Whistling Swan, Irvine 92714

Laura Staben, 1350 Say Rd., Santa Paula 93060

Charlene Stempel, 2707 Michael Dr., Newbury Park 91320

Donna Stephens, Rte. 9, Box 106, Bakersfield 93309

Lavola Stock, 1886 S. Chester, Bakersfield 93302

Beth Stoval, 7427 Genesta Ave., Van Nuys 91406

Diane Strohmeyer, 1105 I St., Petuluma 94952

Lonnie L. Sutter, 1444 Key View, Corona Del Mar 92652

Lois Swarts, 11629 Juniper Hills Rd., Littlerock 93543

Jennie Taylor, 819 Cambon Circle, Ojai 93023

Beverly Thompson, 25 Chateau Lane, Napa 94558

Dixie Thorne, 2205 Maricopa Rd., Ojai 93023

Peggy Thornton, Box 723, Morgan Hills 95037

Clair Torrey, 5819 Morage Ave., Oakland 94611

Pearl Tudor, 59 E. Lewis St., Ventura 93001

Elizabeth J. Turley, 12967 Belfair, Norwald 90650

Kathy Turner, 2292 Newquist Ct., Camarillo 93010

Katherine Valentine, 2302 Redondo Beach Blvd., Torrance 90504

Joyce N. Van Vleet, 4602 Terrance Ave., Oxnard 93030

Peyton Varner, P.O. Box 129, 7759 Happy Canyon Rd., Santa Ynez 93460

Heather Villman, 6620 Mt. Hope Dr., San Jose 95120

Joy Angela Voelkers, 2900 Panama Dr., Bakersfield 93306

Pam Warkentin, 153 Karen Pl., Buellton 93427

Rita Weeks, 11238 Redondo Ct., Cupertino 95014

Florence M. Wheeler, 10840 Aqueduct, Granada Hills 91344

Mary Whitney, 12277 Orizaba Ave., Downey 90242

Kelly Wilbanks, 25603 Fallenleaf Dr., Torrance 90505

Ruth Ann Wise, 1609 Mt. Vernon Dr., Modesto 95350

Jeanne Wray, 24424 Vista Ridge Dr., Valencia 91355

Nancy Ann Yartz, 25372 Adelanto, Laguna Niguel 92677

Pat Yost, 3315 W. Michigan, Stockton 95204

Barbara Young, 1238 Temple Dr., Pachelo 94002

Debbie Young, 2820 Tenaya Dr., Merced 95340

Rhae Young, 2820 Tenaya Dr., Merced 95340

Carolyn S. Ziegler, 1247 Talbryn Dr., Belmont 94002

Colorado

Emma Anderson, 45024 Co. Rd. B, Center 81125

Jean Benzie, 5003 Halfmoon, Colorado Springs 80915

Sheryle Bonnell, 351 Northridge, Grand Junction 81501

Lois Brady, 1265 Olathe St., Aurora 80011

Sr. Mary Imelda Cox, Rte. 3, Box 75, Golden 80401

Linda Dickerson, 8965 Yukon St., Westminster 80020

Donna Eden, 764 Grand Ave., Delta 81416

Ruth Eitel, 8567 Rabbitbrush Way, Parker 80134

Patricia A. Greene, 10520 B. West Fair Ave., Littleton 80127

Dorothy Johnson, Box 9212, Frisco 80443

Patti Kraus, 2713 S. Meade, Denver 80236

Barbara Lee, 2342 Oleander Dr., Loveland 80537

Jean Mackay, 3680 Ames St., Denver 80212

Alberta M. Murray, 13149 W. Ohio Ave., Denver 80226

Barbara Otto, 364-29 Rd., Grand Junction 81501

Eileene Pippinger, 7447 S. Lamar, Littleton 80123

Judy Richards, 5108 S. Nelson, Denver 80123

Marjorie Richardson, 2359 Monument Dr., Grand Junction 81503

Wildie Rife, Star Rte. Box 26, Lamar 81052

Betty Sours, 5153 S. Miller St., Littleton 80123

Jeanne Spencer, 35523 Weld. Co. Rd. 31, Eaton 80615

Karrel Stevens, 3510 Inspiration, Colorado Springs 80917

Alberta Teasley, 5215 Kendrick Ct., Golden 80401

Jana Jo Towery, 3701 Royal Dr., Fort Collins 80526

Carol York, 618 W. Valleyview Ave., Littleton 80120

Connecticut

Sonya Bird, 775 Manchester Rd., Glastonbury 06033

Doris Blodgett, 123 Ridgewood Rd., Wallingford 06492

Joann Braun, 254 Fairfield Woods Rd., Fairfield 06430

Judy Cronan, 384 N. Main St., Union City 06770

Georgia Ferris, 87 Fulling Mill Lane, Ridgefield 06430

Doreen Gammons, 13 Robin Lane, Killingworth 06417

Ruth Ann Greenhill, 51 Platt Lane, Milford 06460

Bertha Guay, Box 111, Rte. 19, Stafford 06075

Jean Hansen, Pettipaug Rd., Box 835, R.R. 2, Westbrook 06498

Esther Hoffman, 184 Rosemere Ave., Fairfield 06432

Marie LeFevre, 20 Millbrook Rd., Stamford 06902

Deanne Pape, 9 Aylesbury Circle, Madison 06443

Joan T. Wadleigh, 15 Oakwood Dr., Gales Ferry 06335

Delaware

Peggy Legg, 11 Warwick Lane, New Castle 19720

Florida

Maxine M. Adams, P.O. Box 295, Baker 32531

Sally Adams, RFD 4, 20 Howard Pl., Saint Augustine 32084

Barbara Anderson, 12775 S.W. 78 Ave., Miami 33156

Jean Archer, 7109 Lauder Pl., Tampa 33617

Shirley Baad, 175 Indian Mound Trail, Tavernier 33070

Estelle Barley, 470 Ninth St., North Naples 33940

Joyce Beebe, 8535 Jade Acres Dr., Pensacola 32506

Pati Bondi, Rte. 7, Box 402-H, Pensacola 32506

Jane Brown, General Delivery, Ponce De Leon 32455

Jane Burkett, 18925 S.W. 248 St., Homestead 33033

Patricia Butler, 7 N.E. 17th Ave., Pompano Beach 33060

Nan Champion, 831 Indian Trail, Destin 32541

Marion Chittenden, 416 Skipper Lane, Port St. Lucie 33498

Vickie Cole, 432 Gregory Ave., Valparaiso 32580

Christine Colley, 2808 E. Strong, Pensacola 32504

B.J. Cook, 4100 W. Kennedy, Tampa 33609

Cheryl Cox, 2610 Citrus Blvd., Haines City 33844

Helen Crawford, 513 Wisconsin Ave., St. Cloud 32769

Sally Croft, Rte. 2, Box 534, Crystal River 32629

Brita Darling, 3025 Huntington Dr., Tallahassee 32303

Betty Denton, 326 Sudduth Circle, Fort Walton Beach 32548

Sally Derby 17104 Inca Ave., Panama City 32407

Charlene Dial, 2206 S. Dale Mabry, Tampa 33609

Julie Dillinger, 701 Overbrook Dr., Fort Walton Beach 32548

Elsie Dunson, 10 Azalea Dr., Mary Esther 32569

Darlyn Finley, 8618 Pluto Terr., Lake Park 33403

Marguerite Fratus, 309 Spanish Moss Trail, Destin 32541

Martha Frenzel, 4617 St. Nazaire Rd., Pensacola 32505

Donna Gay, 3404 Game Farm Rd., Panama City 32405

Margaret Gay, 1918 Wilson Ave., Panama City 32405

Nell Gerry, 3303 Hopkins, Titusville 31780

Marilyn Habbenfeld, 5307 Chippendale Circle, Fort Myers 33907

Gertrude D. Hardin, P.O. Box 881, Tavernier 33070

Marti Harnisch, 804 Darlinton Ct., Fort Walton Beach 32548

Fay Herrington, 2581 Telstar Ave., Orlando 32805

Dee Hesington, 1777 E. Crooked Lake Dr., Eustis 32726

Jane O. Hildebrand, 404 Brentwood Ave., Deland 32720

Dristi Hilzinger, PSC Box 3274, Apo, Miami 32424

Deborah A. Hoelzel, 719 Osceola Circle, Eglin AFB 32542

Margaret Hofsetter, 8325 S.E. 116 Terr., Miami 33156

Ann Jones, Rte. 3, Box 629, Tallahassee 32308

Mary Ann Katch, 4822 S.W. First Ct., Cape Coral 33904

Barbara Lobsinger, 5600 Turin St., Orlando 32807

Mozelle Lord, 1103 N.W. Pink Lake Dr., Stuart 33494

Peggy Maudlin, 2268 N.W. 30th Rd., Boca Raton 33431

Carole McCully, 5631 St. Amatus, Pensacola 32503

Doris Merritt, P.O. Box 192, Lynn Haven 32444

Dorothy Montgomery, 2409 Napoleon Bonaparte, Tallahassee 32308

Jimmy Morrison, 10448 Dodd Rd., Jacksonville 32218

Beverly M. Neligh, P.O. Box 938, Englewood 33533

Beverly Page, 771 S. Longwood Cr., Panama City 32405

Marjan Parker, Rte. 1, Box 1405, Crestview 32536

Sue M. Peacock, Rte. 2, Box 738-4, Crystal River 32629

Helen Petteway, P.O. Box 532, Williston 32696

Elaine Polk, 9471 Wexford Rd., Jacksonville 33903

Linda Price, 8225 Fachom Rd., Pensacola 32504

Nell D. Ransone, 17 Hazzard St., Golfview, West Palm 33406

Verna E. Reich, 5200 N.E. 5th Ave., Fort Lauderdale 33340
Zelma B. Rinehart, 219-9900 Ulmerton Rd., Largo 33541
Norma P. Rossis, Rte. 2, Box 898, Crescent City 32012
Judy Rouse, 22 James Ave., Shalimar 32579
Mary Seeman, 7402 Lake Breeze Dr. S.W., Apt. 212, Fort Myers 33907
Darlene Snyder, 1233 S.E. 10th Ave., Ocala 32670
Lajune Stephens, 2052 S. Jefferson St., Perry 32347
Jeanne Steverson, 1718 Sharon Rd., Tallahassee 32303
Hazel Stills, 1216 West Vine St., Kissimmee 32741
Verna Stroehl, Rte. 1, Box 190-GR, Crestview 32536
Vera Stuckey, 7801 Firestone, Bayonet Point 33567
Glenda C. Thomas, Rte. 2, Box 316, Crystal River 32629
Jackie Thumsen, 152 Point O'Woods Dr., Daytona Beach 32014
Phyllis J. West, 555 Chinquapin Dr., Eglin AFB 32542
Kathy Whiteside, 95 S.E. 7th Ave., Deerfield Beach 33441
Gloria C. Whitman, 45 New Fawn Ct., Safety Harbor 33572
Kathy Wiles, 3920 33rd St. S.E., Rusken 33570
Jerrye Winters, 2036 San Marino Way, Clearwater 33515
Gail Witte, Rte. 1, Box 197 A, Blountstown 32424
Dorothy Wood, 5027 Dorlan Ave., Orlando 32809

Georgia

Charlotte Echols Adams, 1244 Weston Dr., Decatur 30032
Wayne J. Adams, Box C, Hoschton 30548
Hilda Akins, Rte. 1, Chula 31733
Anne Barker, 1477 Gloria St., Griffin 30223
Connie Blair, P.O. Box 605, Byron 31008
Louise Brown, Rockmart Rd., Rte. 1, Cartersville 30120
Mary D. Bruner, Box 705, Blakely 31723
Carroll Byers, 1943 Queens Way, Chamblee 30341
Shirley Chipman, 3223 Ware Rd., Augusta 30909
Elaine Chord, 2440 Cedar Fork Trail, Marietta 30062
Beverlie Chumley, Rte. #2, Cartersville 30120
Addie Davis, 889 Wimbish Rd., Macon 31208
Chelita Freeman, 1067 Sandy Creek Rd., Fayetteville 30214
Nita Garland, 2525 Ward St., J-1, Smyrna 30080
Barbara Geer, 2617 Langland Ct. N.E., Atlanta 30345
Carol Harris, P.O. Box 670, Valdosta 31601
Judith M. Harvey, 738 Beechwood Dr., Savannah 31406
Ruth Herman, Rte. 4, Box 428A, Cleveland 30528
Sharon Johnson, 410 Colbiers Creek Rd., Watkinsville 30677
Laura Lightsey, Rte. 1, Box 258, Bristol 31518
Joyce McClure, 3000 Sylvester Rd., Albany 31705

Ruth Murphy, 1670 Debbie Dr., Mableton 30059
Chris Myer, 3187 Montheath Pass, Duluth 30136
Sylvia V. Novak, 5248 Smokerise Dr., Stone Mountain 30083
Gini Oakes, Rte. 2, Box 126, Young Harris 32805
Valeri O'Neill, Rte. 1, Box 293A, Plainville 30733
June Pendley, P.O. Box 56, Chula 31733
Judith T. Phillips, 5183 Big A Rd., Douglasville 30135
Daisy H. Sargent, Rte. 3, Steadman Rd., Buchanan 30113
Billie U. Stickland, Rte. 2, Box 216, Claxton 30417
Bonnie Sturgis, 2402 Castlewood Dr., Augusta 30904
Pat Turner, 5934 Huntington Dr., Grovetown 30813
Linda Williford, 408 S. Jefferson, Ashburn 31714

Hawaii

Lora Anderson, 500 University Ave., Apt. 1414, Honolulu 96814
Rae Marie Copeland, 204 Third St., Honolulu 96818
Barbara Del Piano, 471 Kapuhulu Ave., Honolulu 96815
Gina McCormick, 333 Uly Niu St., Kailua 96734

Idaho

Louise Comstock, 11250 Eastshore Dr., Hayden Lake 83835
Sharon De Garimore, Box 772, McCall 83638
Bertha Fullmer, 236 S. 1st W., Resburg 83440
Glena Greiner, 534 W. 17th, Burley 83318
Carol J. King, 815 S. Holmes, Idaho Falls 83401
Dottie Nester, Rte. 4, Box 4067, Burley 83318
Muriel Worthylake, Star Rte., Box 290, McCammon 83250

Illinois

Ronda Addison, Box 182, Mackinow 61755
Dorris J. Alm, 1319 W. Concord Lane, Schaumburg 60193
Sandra Aubuchon, 905 N. Cleveland, Effingham 62401
Eloise Baxter, 135 E. Madison, Rushville 62681
Roberta Blick, 18 N. 7th Ave., Saint Charles 60174
Cynthia Borman, 522 Tanglewood Lane, Frankfort 60423
Toni Carbo, 1400 W. 55th Pl., Countryside 60525
Betty Cathcart, 320 South Park, Maressa 62257
Harlene Childress, 562 N. Van Northwick, Batavia 60510

Mamara D. Cowger, Rte. 1, Box 77, Wheeler 62479

Bobbie Cox, 99 Barnes Rd., Harrisburg 62946

Ann Cunningham, 502 S. Vale, Bloomington 61701

Paula Devore, 112 N. 3, P.O. Box 304, Altamont 62411

Gayle Dixon, 4214 O'Connell, Rockford 61109

Jane Dobbs, Rte. 5, Salem Rd., Mt. Vernon 62864

Ardith Dolamore, 146 W. Lemoyne, Lombard 60148

Dawn M. Donald, 203 W. Fast Ave., Mackinow 61755

Bonnie Doty, Rte. 2, Princeton 61356

Norma Edwards, 40 Stacy Ave., Streator 61364

Donna Fahlgren, 904 N. LaPorte, Melrose Park 60161

Angee Fikaris, 160 Burlington, Clarendon Hill 60514

Agnes Gardner, 67 Beth Ann Dr., Belleville 62221

Karen Gehm, 2717 Seventh St., Peru 61354

Opal Green, 3729 Ruth Dr., Granite City 62040

Mitzi Hands, 1593 Surrey Dr., Wheaton 60187

Patricia Harris, Rte. 3, Quincy 62301

Roberta M. Helson, 1 S. 609, Lorraine, Glen Ellyn 60137

Winnie Heuer, 1750 Meadow Lane, Bannockburn 60015

Carole Hill, 1704 W. Gilbert, Peoria 61604

Linda R. Hoelter, 100 E. Saint Paul St., Spring Valley 61362

Shirley Hollingsworth, 511 S. Chicago Ave., Bismarck 61814

Elsie Kelm, 7631 Monroe, Forest Park 60130

Dolores Klippert, 1003 N. Fernandez, Arlington Heights 60004

Sharon Knight, 238 S. Richmond, Westmont 60559

Peggy Legeriet, P.O. Box 163, Metropolis 62960

Sharon McGlasson, 305 Fletcher Hills, Danville 61832

Andrea Medved, 718 Terry, Joliet 60435

Sharon Middleton, 4107 Dean Dr., Decatur 62526

Rita Miller, 1929 Weathersfield Way, Schaumburg 60193

Roberta Miller, 14901 S. Kostner Ave., Midlothian 60445

Murriel Mills, 214 N. Dunton Ave., Arlington Heights 60006

Doris Mook, 1252 State Dr., Alton 62002

Verna Morris, R.R. 1, Jacksonville 62650

Gola Pashon, 2605 McNeill Rd., Rock Falls, 61071

Wilma Noe Payne, R.R. 1, Box 96A, Stewardson 62463

Carol Phillips, Rte. 2, Louisville 62858

Sharron Pirro, 34 W. Wilson, Lombard 60148

Erma Ragle, 4650 Fitzgerald Rd., Decatur 62521

Anne Reynolds, 205 N. Border, Maressa 62257

Gina Richardson, 423 S. Cherry, Centralia 62801

Marsha J. Rosenbalm, 104 S. Eighth St., Oregon 61061

Helen T. Rosing, 906 Boesch Pl., Ingleside 60041

Harriet V. Schultz, 1818 Fairway Ct., Kankakee 60901

Anne Seale, 603 Harris Box 126, Greenville 62246

Lorry Sedlacek, 14213 Rte. 176, Woodstock 60098

Cindy Wallenburg, 4850 W. 85th St., Burbank 60459

Patricia Werthe, 103 S. Lincoln, Batavia 60510

Denise White, Rte. 1, Box 70, Dieterick 62424

Ellen Wiesner, 8531 W. Cermack, North Riverside 60546

Marie Wilson, 1605 White St., Mt. Vernon 62864

Indiana

Linda Albrecht, 1951 Berne Ave., Terre Haute 47805

Sara Baumgardner, 5632 Radnor Rd., Indianapolis 46226

Margaret Berlien, 120 E. Main, Brownsburg 46112

Midge Bond, 4442 N. College Ave., Indianapolis 46205

Diane Burrell, 1712 Shepherd Rd., Anderson 46011

Donna Campbell, 1606 Audubon Rd., Vincennes 47591

Maryhelen Carroll, 2924 E. Cameron St., Indianapolis 46206

Elaine Cioni, 53 W. 68th Pl., Merrillville 46410

Cathy Cohen, Stanton Lake Lot 117, Leesburg 46538

Marilyn R. Copeland, Rte. 1, Box 164, South Whitney 46787

Dawn R. Cornell, 1700 E. First St., Anderson 46012

Barbara M. Dillon, 416 Main, Rockport 47635

Nancy Engledow, 11822 Lancaster Cr., Carmel 46032

Patricia Gray, 7453 Cotherstone Ct., Indianapolis 46206

Maxine Hales, 922 E. Lincoln Dr., Mt. Vernon 47620

Evelyn Kirsch, Box 128, Ambia 47917

Sue Kruger, 1407 Rivercrest, Warsaw 46580

Rosalie Landau, Rte. 1, Box 143, Muncie 47302

Carol LaRue, Rte. 8, Box 207, Warsaw 46580

Roena Preston, 1496 Oldford, New Albany 47150

Karen Roberts, 6625 Finchley Rd., Indianapolis 46206

Anne Roman, 7818 Delcon Dr., Fort Wayne 46801

Ida Russell, 740 Main St., Brookville 47012

Lois Schell, 5648 E. Saugana, Rolling Prairie 46371

Suzie Schmitz, 6455 Kingswood Dr., Indianapolis 46206

Marthy Searcy, 2714 Kaywood, New Albany 47150

Leona Shafer, 5606 Spring Lake Dr., Evansville 47710

Conklin Shelly, P.O. Box 254, West Lebanon 47991

Rosella Sisco, 61194 Locust Dr., South Bend 46624

Amy Stahl, 492 Manor Dr., Seymour 47274

Mary Jane Todd, 1507 Oak Hill Rd., Evansville 47711

Jessie Mae Walker, 408 Seymour Rd., Crothersville 47227

Pat Walker, 2205 Hanover, Indianapolis 46227

Jean Weber, 1306 Bullseye Lake Rd., Valparaiso 46383

Sheila Wiles, 412 Plymouth Rd., Valparaiso 46383

Ellen Wilson, 2800 E. 10th St., Hobart 46342

Jo Wood, 70 W. Market St., Wabash 46992

Iowa

Andrea Bean, Rte. 1, Albert City 50510

Audrey Bettin, R.R. 2, Odebolt 51458

Eileen Blaskovich, Rte. 1, Box 131, Lohrville 51453

Dorothy Boeckmann, 902 Second Ave. N.E., Waverly 50677

Kathryn Brandon, Box 144, Logan 51546

Maxine Citta, 2201 7th St., Harlan 51537

Margaret Clayton, 2622 Beaver Ave., Des Moines 50301

Renee Driscoll, R.R. 3, Box 71, Williamsburg 52361

Janet Edgar, 769 Cody Dr., Dubuque 52001

Bernice Fullhart, 303 Westwood Dr., Ames 50010

Donna Good, 8383 University, Des Moines 50301

Katie Gorsuch, 701 Third Ave. S.E., Cedar Rapids 52406

Alleen Hedge, R.R. 1, Fremont 52561

Shirley Johnstone, 10 W. 4th, Spencer 51301

Mildred Karber, W. Main, Grand Junction 50157

Trellis Kitt, R.R. 2, Sac City 50583

Sheryl Kuiper, R.R. 1, Archer 51231

Patrician Leddon, P.O. Box 87, Scarville 50473

Faye A. Lenz, R.R. 2, Wapello 52653

Ruth Mosher, 712 S.E. Magazine Rd., Ankeny 50021

Marcella Nicol, 512 Cedar Bend, Waterloo 50703

Carol Ann Stiers, 301 Kirkwood, Iowa City 52240

Joyce Streeter, 20 S. Main Ave., Britt 50423

Vi Thurmond, 343 S.E. Miller, Des Moines 50301

Julie Van Cleave, R.R. 1, Perry 50220

Ruby Weber, Cedarcrest Rd., Columbus Junction 52738

Joan White, 500 Acres, Burlington 52601

Carol Whitters, Rte. 2, Cedar Rapids 52406

Louise Wiley, Rte. 2, Carlisle 50047

Kansas

Joan Allen, Rte. 1, Box 14A, Chetopa 67336

Myrtice Audiss, 730 Sheeran, Chapman 67431

Carol Bennett, 8221 Grandview, Overland Park 66204

Lois Black, 546 W. Main, Valley Center 67147

Mary Ann Bowie, P.O. Box 393, Douglas 67039

Sue Jean Brooks, 1301 Stewart, Winfield 67156

Kay Campbell, 9316 W. 77 Terr., Overland Park 66204

Margaret Carlson, 513 N. Lincoln, Liberal 67901

Mary Channell, P.O. Box 173, Hanston 67849

Lucille Clark, 1003 Apache, Wichita 67202

Lois Cooper, 3401 Hillcrest Rd., Independence 67301

Lois Cranor, 120 N. First St., Independence 67301

Virginia Cranston, 9 Rambler Rd., Hutchinson 67501

Jan Forsyth, 209 S. Walnut, Medicine Lodge 67104

Jerg Frogley, 502 Fifth, Oswego 67356

Beverly Goble, 2105 Prairie Lane, Emporia 66801

Susan Ann Green, P.O. Box 8, Burns 66840

Lorraine Hadsell, 626 E. Main, Marion 66861

Mary Haltom, 14 E. Second St., Hutchinson 67501

Vera Harms, Box 128, Thayer 66776

Alice Higdon, 7612 Warren, Wichita 67201

Barbara House, 1349 High Dr., McPherson 67460

Lucy Moffat, 1220 Taft, Great Bend 67530

Clara Murry, 603 N. 8th, Box 606, Garden City 67846

Dane Normile, Denton 66017

Katherine Oltjen, R.R. 1, Everest 66424

Maxine Rauscher, P.O. Box 184, Goodland 67735

Carolyn Sayler, 1107 Harding, Garden City 67846

Sandy Shields, 14 Century Pkwy., Neodesha 66757

Joan Shortes, 408 E. 5th, Oswego 67356

Bettie J. Sitts, Rte. 12, 203 Ninnescah, Kingman 67068

Judith Steffen, 1221 W. 14th St., Chanute 66720

J. Norma Webert, R.R. 1, Box 200, Salina 67401

Connie Weibe, Rte. 4, Box 1836, Coffeyville 67337

Georgia Westhoff, 2801 Main, Parsons 67357

Betty Wick, 313 A. St., Abilene 67410

Kentucky

Marguerite Baker, Rural Route, Beechmont 42323

Anna Lois Beumel, 1705 Morningside Dr., Owensboro 42301

Jo Crary, 70 Orchard Hill, Fort Thomas 41075

Jewel Dean Ford, 1010 Legion Park Rd., Greensburg 42743

Verna Heltzel, 2517 Cox Mill Rd., Hopkinsville 42240

Harriett Jones, 2370 Edwards Mill Rd., Hopkinsville 42240

Gayle Laible, 478 Kuhrs Lane, Covington 41012

Una Mayhew, 1428 Laurel Ave., Bowling Green 42101

Lessie Moreno, 232 Indiana Trail, Radcliffe 40160

Louise Shelton, 2901 Thistlewood Dr., Louisville 40206

Mary Sowell, 111 Park Lane Dr., Paducah 42001

Louisiana

Peggy T. Avault, 1058 Oak Hills Pkwy., Baton Rouge 70810

Dorsey E. Barnes, 2236 Williamsburg, La Place 70068

Deena Blanchard, 200 Chastant Blvd., Lafayette 70508

Janice Buras, 106 Braye Dr., Buras 70041

Patricia Buras, P.O. Box 456, Buras 70041
Eileen Cannon, 1153 Ashland Dr., Baton Rouge 70806
Faye Drobnic, P.O. Box 984, 505 Main St., Patterson 70392
Zella Duncan, 822 Shady Lane, Westlake 70669
Debbie Folse, 112 Barrios St., Lockport 70374
Judy Folse, 112 Barrios St., Lockport 70374
Myriam Harmon, 130 E. Randall Ct., Gretna 70053
Marverine Hickman, 245 Brookwood Dr., Woodworth 71485
Sandy Hogan, 3719 Greenway Pl., Shreveport 71105
Bonnis Hoskin, Rte. 1, Box 20, Buras 70041
Barbara Houser, 53 Winchester, Monroe 71203
Ophelia Lefort, P.O. Box 588, Larose 70373
Elizabeth Lott, Rte. 2, Box 912, Elm Grove 71051
Kay McCrabb, 5118 Dogwood Dr., Houghton 71037
Janie Mistich, Box 314, Buras 70041
Leta Mock, Rte. 2, Box 63, Lecompte 71246
Emmy Lou Montgomery, 1367 W. Jefferson, Lake Charles 70605
Joyce Oldham, 1103 Rathburn, Minden 71055
Marilyn Oliver, 3603 Royce Dr., Alexandria 71303
Betty Partier, P.O. Box 397, Lutchen 70071
Patricia Price, 303 Benville St., Winnfield 71483
Gayle Bass Robinson, 4040 Huntwick, Alexandria 71301
Betty S. Swearingen, 8739 Jefferson, Baton Rouge 70616
Judith Teague, 6039 Gaylyn Dr., Shreveport 71102
Polly Waldron, 2208 Briarmont St., Monroe 71301
Myrna Waters, P.O. Box 369, Larose 70373
Barbara Welch, 3728 Momosa Ct., New Orleans 70114
Connie White, 176 Oakwood, Mandeville 70448
Betty L. Woodhead, Box 517, Sterlington 71280

Maine

Lyndas Country Craft, 143 Water St., Skowhegan 04976
Mona Ridley, R.R. 1, Waldoboro 04572

Maryland

Nancy Clark, 220 Randolph Rd., Silver Springs 20875
Linda Dickinson, 6126 Bell Station Rd., Glenn Dale 20769
Linda B. Foote, 8510 Goodluck Rd., Lanham 20801
Margaret E. Glass, 7617 Carteret Rd., Bethesda 20034
Marilyn Knight, 12146 Long Ridge Lane, Bowie 20715
Juanita Marsh, 1704 Fallway Dr., Crofton 21114

Beverly Martin, 331 Wende Way, Glen Burnie 21061
Roberta P. Maushardt, 8204 Peach Orchard Rd., Dundalk 21222
Helen Randles, 15321 Narcissus Way, Rockville 20853
Marilynne Robertson, 17440 Naylor Rd., Sabillasville 21780
Toni Simonis, 13609 Russett Terr., Rockville 20853
Iva C. Wessinger, 6807 Picnic Woods Rd., Middletown 21769

Massachusetts

Judy Arsenault, 339 Chestnut, Gardner 02440
Lisa M. Babcock, Ross Hill Rd., Bradford 02808
Irene E. Bedard, 5 Plymouth Blvd., Westport 02790
Nancy Bock, 63 Wenham Rd., Topsfield 01983
Mary Boganno, 6 Mann St., Braintree 02184
Claire S. Casperson, 1 Indian Hill Rd., Burlington 01803
Joyce Dipasquale, 1 Gladwalt Rd., Northboro 01532
Joanne Dzengielewski, 30 Washburn St., Dorchester 02125
Ethel Hannabury, 129 Porter St., Melrose 02176
Dorothy M. Johnson, 176 Hunt Rd., Chelmsford 01824
Julie Kelly, 88 River Rd., Norfolk 02056
Vellis King, 13 Spring St., North Brookfield 01535
Sylvia Kondelka, 666 Montgomery Rd., Westfield 01085
Madeleine Lucier, 54 Wilson St., Spencer 01562
Gene Mahoney, 1166 Main St., Hingham 02034
Carol Ann McGrath, 1 Fountain St., Billerica 01821
Helen A. Owens, 390 Southbridge St., Auburn 01501
Ann Patsis, 203 Grove St., Worcester 01605
Jean Reader, 12 The Great Rd., Bedford 02730
Marilyn Rich, 9 Weathers Lane, Bolton 01740
Katherine Ryan, 191 Westwood Ave., East Longmeadow 01028
Bette St. Martin, 397 Main, Fitchburg 01420
Alice Smith, 523 N. Westfield, Feeding Hill 01030
Joan Sprague, 491 Prospect St., East Longmeadow 01028
Patricia Susanecki, 50 Brookside Dr., Wilbraham 01095
Patricia A. Tanguay, 24 Ashland Ave., Methuen 01844
Eula Tolman, 32 Robinhood Rd., Natick 01760
Marianne Trepanier, 308 Mass. Ave., North Andover 01845
Katharine Turnblom, 100 Greenwood, Worcester 01607
Constance Turner, 37 Washington, Reading 01867
Jeane Weeks, 8 Lee St., Lancaster 01523
Suzanne Weise, 6 Whittier Rd., Milford 01757
Muriel Woodruff, 76 Orange St., Reading 01867
Lorraine Wrenn, 29 Crabtree Rd., Plymouth 02360
Yvonne Wright, 580 North Central, Winchendon 01475

Michigan

Doris Austin, Rte. 2, 62nd St., Hartford 49087

Jean G. Barlett, 103 E. Colby St., Whitehall 49461

Joanne Bellmard, 121 S. Thompkins St., Howell 48843

Sue Bouchard, 1875 Camile S.E., Grand Rapids 49506

Kitty Briand, 42464 Somerset Ct., Canton 48187

Glenna Briggs, 960 Capital Ave., Battle Creek 49017

Rosemary Briski, 1058 Blairmoor, Grosse Pointe Woods 48236

Ardath Burry, 931 Vine St., Adrian 49221

Karen Coleman, 6155 S. Sheridan, Muskegon 49444

June E. Cox, 24224 W. 7 Mile 69, Detroit 48219

Rose A. Daly, 16729 Fenmore, Detroit 48235

Patricia DeFaldo, 11576 Brownell, Plymouth 48170

Pat Degraw, 224 Michael Ave., Shepherd 48883

Doris Dickson, 39649 Moravian Dr., Mount Clemens 48043

Kerry Dorstewitz, Rte. Box 451, Watervliet 49098

Mary L. Ellis, 5385 Pointe Dr., Marine City 48039

Thelma M. Erway, 11031 Hastings Point Rd., Middleville 49333

Gloria Fedoruk, 17144 Englewood, Allen Park 48101

Peggy R. Ferrari, 15667 Blue Skies, Livonia 48154

Marie Fowler, 9550 S. Luce, Perrinton 48871

Jo An Frent, 32726 Winona Ct., Westland 48185

Christy Gorrow, 8401 18 Mile #54, Sterling Heights 48078

Roberta Goupil, Rte. 2, Box 512A, Houghton Lake 48629

Jean L. Guenther, 1424 Birchrest Dr., Dearborn 48124

June Hackbarth, 1205 Scott St., Midland 48640

Esther J. Hasbrouck, 2220 Bryon Rd., Howell 48843

Judith Henderson, 6032 Higgins, Sterling Heights 48078

Betsy Ann Hill, 1033 107th Ave., Plainwell 49080

Dorothy Johnson, 6851 Rosemary, Dearborn Heights 48127

Dawn Kapp, 7780 Chichester, Canton 48187

Marie Kimsey, 2715 N. Fifth St., Kalamazoo 49009

Sharon Kneshtel, 3285 Humber, Trenton 48183

Nikki Le Clair, 432 M-SS, Tawas City 48763

Kathy Ahrens Leverett, 15869 Sussex, Detroit 48227

Florence Lossing, 600 S. Fowlerville Rd., Fowlerville 48836

Cynthia L. Lowrie, 2923 Cooper Ave., Port Huron 49060

Peggy Mack, 31711 Olmstead, Rockwood 48173

Jean Meek, 2825 Ironwood Dr., Jackson 49201

Patricia Mifsud, 111 Brentwood, Dearborn 48124

Linda Miller, 1335 E. Grand River, Portland 48875

Nita Montgomery, 15325 Reeck, Southgate 48195

Helen Morgan, 930 Lakeview, Portage 49081

Marilyn J. Pagels, 10070 Sprinkle Rd., Vicksburg 49097

Patricia Petro, 11523 E. Bath Rd., Byron 48418

Mary Lou Raftery, 1127 U.S. 31, P.O. Box 254, Petoskey 49770

Sharon Richards, 9988 Inkster, Redford 48239

Joyce E. Richter, 4801 S. Cedar, Lansing 48910

Maureen F. Ryan, 18 Spokane Dr., Pontiac 48053

Muriel Salata, 14336 Henry Ruff, Livonia 48154

Jackie V. Sanderson, 52 E. Jefferson, Quincy 49082

Judy Schneider, 201 N. Riverside, Saint Clair 48079

Pat Seay, 605 Adrian St., Tecumseh 49286

Priscilla Shaffner, 19500 Hilton, Southfield 48075

Margaret Skrobat, 274 Fairway Ct., Plainwell 49080

Jan Smith, 48761 I-94 Serv. Dr., Belleville 48111

Velda Jean Smith, 1482 Cahoun Rd., Addison 49220

Gladys Spence, 7773 Macomb, Grosse Ile 48138

Karen Stark, 868 E. Chicago Rd., Quincy 49082

Sharon Stoeckel, 1496 Roslyn Rd., Grosse Pointe Woods 48236

Jan Strickland, 10301 Brodhead, Grosse Ile 48138

Joann Stringari, 21462 Wedgewood Dr., Detroit 48236

Pat Szukhent, 913 Birchwood Dr., Flushing 48433

Rosalie Szukhent, 7149 Grenada, Flint 48504

Amy Venhoven, 300 W. 28th, Holland 49423

Diana Ware, 1812 E. Ashman St., Midland 48640

Lynette B. Wells, 1005 Carlton Blvd., Jackson 49201

Mary E. Whitlow, 4065 Waldon Rd., Lake Orion 48035

Betty Wichman, 9980 N. Tittawaw Assee, Freeland 49623

Jean Willits, 17738 Kinloch, Redford 48240

Elouise "Pud" Wilson, 406 Park Ave., Yale 48097

Minnesota

Rita Kay Bakke, 900 S. Second, Marshall 56258

Marian Bestor, P.O. Box 303, Rochester 55960

Charlene Brose, 11566 Bailey, Woodburg 55055

Karen Clarke, 7138 Angus Ave., Inver Grove Heights 55076

Joyce C. Cody, 109 Howard St., Hibbing 55746

Eileen Conrow, 3302 Kentwood Ct., Burnsville 55337

Donna Gould, 815 S. 10th St., Moorehead 56560

Norma Hallisey, R.R. 6, Box 75, Fergus Falls 56537

Helen Halstead, Rte. 2, Box 150, Brooten 56316

Florence Hasbarger, R.R. 3, Jewett Lake, Fergus Falls 56537

Norrine Howard, 16096 6th St. N., Lakeland 55043

Glenace Metcalfe, R.R. 3, Box 736-C, Pelican Rapids 56537

Joyce Morsching, 6380 Glen Rd., Newport 55055

Shirley Olsen, 1425 Eighth Ave. N., Saint Cloud 56301

Kay Portz, 814 N. Grace St., Saint Peters 56082

Linda Quist, 810 5th Ave. S.E., Rte. 3, Pipestone 56164

Mary Ralston, 720 S. Miller, Litchfield 55355

Barbara J. Smith, 911 W. Summit, Fergus Falls 56537
Joy Smith, Plaza Square Center, Winona 55987
Rebecca Thomas, Forest Manor Addition, Saint Joseph 56374
Marabeth Timmers, 1621 E. Sandhurst Dr., Saint Paul 55109
Dianne Verba, Rte. 2, Box 30, Sauk Centre 56378
Sandra Walker, Box 118, Oronoco 55960
Ann Jackson Wright, 819 S.E. 9th Ave., Faribault 55021

Mississippi

Barbara Allen, Rte. 3, Box 566, Gulfport 39503
Jo Anne Ashcraft, Box 1411, Greenwood 38930
Carolyn Boone, 215 Eastwood Dr., Columbus 39701
Ruth Buck, 12404 Cambridge Blvd., Ocean Springs 39564
Dell Cooper, Rte. 1, Box 226, Poplarville 39470
Sue Dees, 13 Kimball, Gulfport 39501
Martha Edwards, 414 Wood St., Water Valley 38965
Betty Flurry, 2 Pecan Wood Cove, Long Beach 39560
Delia Green, Rte. 6, Box 153RR, Hattiesburg 39401
Pat Harris, Rte. 1, Box 244, Toomsuba 39301
Gerri Hughes, 1214 Winterview Dr., Jackson 39204
Liz Lumpkin, 1750 Maria Dr., Jackson 39204
Bernadette M. Mabry, 703 Emerald Lane, Hattiesburg 39401
Edna Manley, 3420 55th Pl., Meridian 39301
Barbara McBride, Rte. 1, Box 705, Florence 39073
Jane McWilliams, 2405-51 St. Ave., Meridian 39301
Georgia Nagorka, Box 188, Lumberton 39445
Beckye Robbins, Rte. 7, Box 393, Hattiesburg 39401
Karen M. St. John, 155 W. Chalson Ave., Holly Springs 38635
Mona Lisa Santiago, 416 St. Jude St., P.O. Drawer 9, Waveland 39576
Mary Lou Stephens, Rte. 12, 518 Maple Dr., Hattiesburg 39401
Jean Tolbert, P.O. Box 1002, Brookhaven 39601
Ann Turner, 6005 Woodhaven Rd., Jackson 39204
Alice Warriner, Rte. 5, Box 204, Poplarville 39470
Judith Warriner, Rte. 5, Box 204, Poplarville 39470

Missouri

Sarah Bateman, 49 Wheeler, Fort Leonard Wood 65473
Beverly Beckmeyer, Box 69, Eureka 63025
Bettie Bollinger, 365 Nancy Lane, Cape Girardeau 63701
Sandra Lee Cashion, 508 Center, Farmington 63640
Jean Crocker, 208 N. Couling, Desloge 63601
Winnie Essmyer, Rte. 2, Box 384, Cape Girardeau 63701
Judith Flowers, 6011 Gaitling Dr., St. Louis 63129
Natalie Groth, 463 Briarwyck Dr., Ballwin 63011
Averial Hartsock, 4101 E. Haverill, Saint Joseph 64506
Bernadine Kirks, Box 102, R.R. 1, Maryville 64468
Margie Larson, Star Rte. 4, Box 201, Houston 65483
Patricia Lowry, 10609 Twilight, St. Louis 63128
Myrtle Mayfield, Rte. 2, Box 299, Sikeston 63801
Marianne McLafferty, 415 Golthe, Kirkwood 63122
Jayne Meyer, 1820 W. McCarty, Jefferson 65101
Betty Milam, Box 114, Benton 63736
Fae Montgomery, 206 S. Main, De Soto 63020
Francis C. Nash, Rte. 3, Box 438, Sunrise Beach 65079
Billie J. Newcomb, 628 Woodland, Moberly 65270
Marjorie Packard, Rte. 4, Box 32, Cameron 64429
Judy Perkins, Rte. 2, Box 48, Bernie 63822
Burton L. Picht, 106 E. Illinois, Box 266, Kirksville 63501
Frankie Polleschultz, 18 Club Grounds S. Drive, Florrisant 63032
Betty Pollock, 115 Missouri, Charleston 63834
Dolores Revelle, 204 Nineteenth Ave., Greenwood 64034
Janice Rosenburg, 1704 Little Brennan Rd., High Ridge 63049
Ann Russell, Rte. 9, Box 506D, Springfield 65801
Lynn Sadler, 802 S. Fible, Kirksville 63501
Wanda Schmidt, 801 Ninth St., Highland 63249
Delores Short, 515 Main, Joplin 64801
Elizabeth Stevens, P.O. Box 26, Gravois Mills 65037
Joan Trant, 444 Briarwyck Dr., Ballwin 63011
Pat Umbach, 4421 Mills St., Independence 64055
Nita Waxelman, 215 W. 13th, Cassville 65625
Judith Wilken, 1502 S. Warren, Sedalia 65301
Susan Woods, 346 Cooperstown Dr., Chesterfield 63017
Katherine Yoss, 123 E. Fourth St., Appleton City 64724
Diane Zimmermann, Rte. 2, Box 177C, Wentzville 63385

Montana

Karen Adams, 18055 Houle Creek Rd., Frenchtown 59834
Brenda Bair, 229 Central Ave., Whitefish 59937
Michele Tebay, Rte. 1, Whitehall 59859

Nebraska

Peggy L. Caauwe, 306 N. Hickory St., Norfolk 68701
Doris Cronin, 447 S. Fourth St., Burwell 68823

Bonnie Distad, 2769 Franklin, Lincoln 68502
Marilyn Dye, Rte. 8, Lincoln 68506
Mary Gillespie, 1334 N. Hickory, Wahoo 68066
Barbara F. Jorgensen, Rte. 1, Box 135, Cozad 69130
Coralen Keeler, 630 W. Ellsworth, Box 171, Arlington 68002
Donna Kruse, Rte. 2, Albion 68620
Marlene La Chapelle, 6623 Bedford Ave., Omaha 68109
Kay McCrabb, Rte. 2, Box 133, Hastings 68901
Val Milbourn, 2970 31st Ave., Columbus 68601
Mildred Pagels, 141 W. 12th St., Fremont 68025
George Rasmussen, 2039 Fair Acre, Fremont 68025
Eleanor B. Schroer, No. 6 Meadowlark, Kearney 68847
Meryl Stortz, 530 Glenhaven Dr., Lincoln 68505
Irene Summers, 8053 Blondo, Omaha 68134
Alice A. Thompson, P.O. Box 6013, Lincoln 68506
Marjorie Thompson, Rte. 1, Archer 68816
Lois C. Tollefsen, 2005 13th Ave., Kearney 68847
Mildred Winkelbauer, Rte. 1, Norfolk 68701

Nevada

E. "Frankie" Brooks, 4184 Candle Berry Ct., Las Vegas 89103
Ivan Brooks, 4184 Candle Berry Ct., Las Vegas 89103
Chris Burkham, 952 Hillside Dr., Elko 89801
Zella Coleman, 143 N. Ronald Lane, Las Vegas 89110
Dawna Daniels, 871 Daniel Dr., Reno 89509
Dorothy Hammond, 3200 Arville #6, Las Vegas 89102
Kay Loudon, 2515 Pioneer Dr., Reno 89509
Gail Meyer, 3864 Chutney, Las Vegas 89121
Sandy Sadler, 1040 Keystone, Reno 89501

New Hampshire

Alayne Abbot, 21 Pako Ave., Keene 03431
Ann Hogan Caine, 283 Pine Hill Rd., Hollis 03049
Ginny Dandreta, 1 Moeckel Rd., Windham 03087
Beverly Desbiens, 16 Nashua Rd., P.O. Box 205, Pelham 03076
Pauline E. Hogan, 16 Alvirne Dr., Hudson 03051
Barbara Laperle, R.F.D. 1, Box 120B, Colebrook 03576
Barbara Madden, Rte. 109, Box 261, Melvin Village 03850
Evelyn V. Mazierz, 4 Tumblebrook Lane, Nashua 03060
Patricia M. Metivier, 2 Sandy Circle, Pelham 03076
Barbara Mone, 43 Charles St., Farmington 03835
Barbara Perkins, 82 Cambridge Rd., Bedford 03102

Marion Pond, R.F.D. 1, Exeter 03833
Terry Provencher, 6 Fogarty Rd., Barrington 03825
Frances Valley, 6 Sunset Dr., Sommersworth 03878
Lucyann Wing, 54 Beaver Lane, Bedford 03102

New Jersey

Sharon Blair, P.O. Box 172, Main St., Califon 07830
Margaret Byrne, 59 Lenox Rd., Summit 07901
Marion Castiglia, 106 Juniper St., Burlington 08016
Barbara Eng, 62 Old Post Rd., Freehold 07728
Angel Forschinbo, 1 Willow Way, Wanaque 07465
Ruth Henshaw, 442 N. 16th St., Kenilworth 07033
Bonnie Litorja, 59 Megill Circle, Eatontown 07724
Roberta Linn Miller, 645 Howard Ave., Pitman 08071
Delores A. Oliver, 8 Cedar Dr., Turnersville 08012
Selma Sellers, 11 Forman Dr., Hamilton Square 08690
Kathleen Stingle, 1215 Wyndmoor Rd., Cherry Hill 08034
Patricia Wehr, 16 Hinchman Ave., Denville 07834
Isabell Wiss, 291 Ridge Rd., North Arlington 07032

New Mexico

Stephanie Ballard, 255 Montgomery Plaza, Albuquerque 87108
Ann Filkins, 8700 Supreme Court, Albuquerque 87111
Pat Greer, 116 W. Pueblo, Hobbs 88240
B.J. Hooe, 1020 E. Amador, Las Cruces 88001
Katy Lindberg, Box 2125, Farmington 87401
Patsy Liston, Rte. 1, Box 130, Clovis 88101
Nancy Posz, 803 Pearson Dr., Roswell 88201

New York

Irene Adams, 842 Forest Ave., Fulton 13069
Lynn Boink, 716 Oswego St., Liverpool 13088
Bette Breen, 111 Shoreway Dr., Rochester 14612
Judith Craddock, 163 Siegel Blvd., Babylon 11702
Marga Dice, 19B Wilson Rd., West Point 10996
Maru Divirgilio, 311 Vandervoort St. N., Tonawanda 14120
Yvonne Dugan, 8473 N. Main, Eden 14057
Carol Empet, 983 W. Dryden Rd., Freeville 13068
Linda Fanniff, 30 Manchester Dr., Clifton Park 12056
Marilee Gilliland, 230 Lincoln Ave., Rochester 14611
Estelle M. Hawkins, 16 Beechwood Ave., Ballston 12019

Rita Hill, Box 177 Penn. Ave., Apalachin 13732

Jean Imgamells, 3278 S. Creek Rd., Hamburg 14075

Sylvia Kelly, 8826 Country Line Rd., Glen Falls 12801

Shirley M. Kent, 7656 E. Dead Creek Rd. Baldwinsville 13027

Nancy Lavender, R.D. 1, Box 215, Plattsburgh 12901

Paula Lawton, R.D. 2, Box 8R, Valatie 12184

Jean Linnard, 39 Brookwood Dr., Latham 12110

Dianne Longmuir, 113 E. Bloomfield St., Rome 13440

Barbara H. Marshall, Box 259, Spruce Lane, Clinton Corners 12514

Karen Marx, 4864 Juneway Dr. S., Liverpool 13088

Ann Murphy, 3560 Carmen Rd., Middleport 14105

Barbara Perkins, 11 Profile Dr., Merrimack 13154

Dottie Phillips, 122 Fairview Ave., Painted Post 14870

Mary Pysz, 27 Donald Dr., North Tonawanda 14120

Laurrel D. Sahagian, 144 Consaul Rd., Albany 12205

Peg Schister, 9 Caveson Lane, Albany 12205

Betty Severtson, R.D. 5, Jamestown 14701

Christine Shields, 6 Old Little Britain Rd., Newburg 12550

Janet Snell, 1273 Pembroke Ct., Schenectady 12309

Shea Szachara, 2850 Vestal Pky W., Vestal 13732

Weitzman's Photo Shop, 61 Canal St., Staten Island 10304

North Carolina

Paulette Adams, 1720 H. Francislan, Winston-Salem 27107

Carol M. Aitken, 5632 Starkwood Dr., Charlotte 28212

Janet Bowen, 3313 Warwick Dr., Jamestown 27282

Donna Carpenter, Rte. 2, Box 106C, Old Fort 28762

Ann S. Davis, Rte. 1, Box 246, Andrews 28901

Margaret Deren, Rte. 1, Box 401, Andrews 28901

Louise Edwards, 508 S. Pine, Rocky Mount 27801

Carolyn Ericson, 6511 Ciscayne Pl., Charlotte 28211

Jimmie Evans, Star Rte., Bat Cave 28710

Regina Ann Ferguson, P.O. Box 61, Hickory Lane, Mineral Springs 28108

Margaret Garner, Rte. 4, 106 Fairway Rd., Morehead City 28557

Barbara Hanson, 1675 Glengarry Dr., Cary 27511

Loretta House, 2853 Reynolds Rd., N.W., Winston-Salem 27106

Alice Johnson, P.O. Box 1029, Shelby 28150

Jon Kovach, 707 W. Aycock St., Raleigh 27608

Alice Morales, 1316 Circle S. Ranch Rd., Monroe 28110

Patty Norwood, 1208 Dove St., Monroe 28110

Lee Schandler, 50 Broadway, Asheville 28807

Louise Schlachter, 5330 Carmel Park Dr., Charlotte 28226

Mary Spainhour, Box 141, Pinnacle 27043

Mildred Whittington, 612 S. Cannon Blvd., Kannapolis 28081

North Dakota

Elsie Colerick, 2016 Selkirk Pl., Rapid City 57701

Millie Ericksen, 609 E. Fourth, Colten 57018

Penny R. Frey, Rte. 1, Jamestown 58401

Linda Lennie, 708 N. 21st, Bismarck 58501

Laura Quaglia, 908 21st N.W., Minot 58701

Judy Rockenback, 2119 Saint Benedict Dr., Bismarck 58501

Barbara J. Ronningen, 1610 16th St. S., Fargo 58103

Susan Stinar, 1601 N. Third St., Grand Forks 58201

Donna Suther, 903 Third St., Britton 57430

Ohio

Audrey Aeschbacher, 1112 Mt. Vernon Ave., Marion 43302

Pattie Anderson, 3163 Easton Rd., Norton 42203

Mildred W. Beacham, 11822 Glenfalls, Cincinnati 45246

Kathy Beaman, 0113 County Rd. 92, Alger 45812

Margaret Beard, 2400 Mechanicsburg Rd., Springfield 45503

Sylvia Bosserman, 623 Spring St., Covington 45318

Bonnie Burkholder, 175 W. Third St., Mansfield 44902

Elaine Clark, 1589 Berkshire Rd., Columbus 43216

Anna Croushore, 5165 Fishburg Rd., Dayton 45401

Carole Donnelly, 4405 N. Bank Rd. N.E., Millerport 43046

Erika Fedderke, 1 Zimmerman Ct., Defiance 43512

Judy Figley, Rte. 6, Defiance 43512

Betty Garratt, 1300 Shrine Rd., Box 147, Springfield 44501

Patricia Grubb, 3256 Bradford, Cleveland Heights 44118

Jean Hablitzel, 10559 Avenue Rd., Perrysburg 43551

Doris Hagensick, 423 S. Arch, Fremont 43420

Alice Hall, 6787 Shurz Rd., Middleton 45042

Marjorie Henheimer, 2435 Hunz Rd., Galloway 43119

Betty Hidy, 123 E. Main St., Donnelsville 45319

Carol Hoffman, 111 E. McPherson Hwy., Clude 43410

Mary Jarnagin, 5915 Gilmore Dr., Fairfield 45014

Deborah Jessee, 811 Picket Way, Cincinnati 45245

Peggy Jessee, 823 Picket Way, Cincinnati 45245

Lois Knight, 2901 Lookout Dr., Zanesville 43701

Agnes Kulchock, 826 Bonnie Brae N.E., Warren 44484

Jo Lamancusa, 565 Broadway, Bedford 44139

Carol D. Martin, 84 Day Ave., Newark 43055

Normagene Martin, 1474 W. State, Rte. 178, Troy 45373

Jo Ann McDevitt, 1672 Ranch Rd., East Palestine 44413

Margarette McDonnell, 380 Mt. Vernon Rd., Newark 43055

Mary Mitro, 178 Saint Mary's St., Norwalk 44857

Nancy Mohr, 39215 Detroit, Avon 44101

Judi Myers, 403 Red Rock Dr., Wadsworth 44281

Tina Norris, 3567 S. Ridge, Perry 44081

Nadine Oldfield, 5360 Vandermarck Rd., Medina 44256

Ruth Orwig, 5540 Bazetta Rd., Cortland 44410

Barbara Pancost, P.O. Box 283, Rte. 700, Hiram 44234

Patricia Paul, 930 Valley View Dr., Brookfield 44403

Sara Payne, 148 High St., Chagrin Falls 44022

Virginia Phillips, Box 23, 223 Northwood Dr., Yellow Springs 45387

Jacqueline Pollack, 4116 Kinsey Rd., Englewood 45332

Sharon Putman, 128 Tolowa Trail, Lima 45802

Nancy Richardson, 3104 Bonnie Villa Lane, Dayton 45431

Marjorie Savely, 100 W. North St., Waverly 45690

Kathryn L. Schreuder, 1905 N. Billman Rd., Genoa 43430

Barbara Schultz, 269 Hager St., Hubbard 44425

Jane Seelig, 24 N. State St., Westerville 43801

Sharon D. Shafer, 330 S. Blanchard, Findlay 45840

Marlo Sigler, 103 S. Main St., Union 45332

Janice Small, 7771 Miller Rd., Greenville 45331

Terry Smith, 12554 Harold Dr., Chesterland 44026

Virginia L. Smith, 1791 Douglas Ave., Monroe 45050

Marjorie Spahr, 585 Highland Park Dr., Akron 44310

Barbara Sturgeon, 701 Crestmont Dr., Dayton 45431

Fran Thompson, 680 Martha Drive S.E., Vienna 44473

Cindi Townsend, 8588 Center St., Garretsville 44231

Evelyn Vicol, 4424 N. Ridge W., Ashtabula 44044

Rita Warner, 4105 Albon Rd., Monclova 43542

Shirley Warren, Rte. 1, Lakeview 43331

Marge Wennerstrom, 5864 Mayfield Rd., Cleveland 44101

Kathy White, Main St. Studios, P.O. Box 75, Lakeview 43331

Martha L. Wick, 4511 Frederick Rd., Dayton 45401

Phyllis J. M. Wogoman, P.O. Box 102, Brookville 45309

Carolyn Wolfe, 434 Whittlesey Dr., Tallmadge 44278

Grace A. Woods, P.O. Box 142, Millersburg 44654

Lois Wyant, 331 E. Lytle 5 Point Rd., Dayton 45459

Floris Zimmerman, 236 W. Liberty St., Wooster 44691

Oklahoma

Gaylene Anglin, 1205 E. 4th St., Stillwater 74074

Virginia Ashley, P.O. Box 789, Marianna 73260

Alice Bearden, 1307 Hickory, Duncan 73633

Marilyn J. Belyeu, WSR Box 260A, Checotah 74426

Jean N. Betler, 420 N. 11th, Fairview 73737

Debby Boss, 9705 S. 235th E. Ave., Broken Arrow 74012

Patty Butler, 2716 S. Bush Ave., Broken Arrow 74012

Gretchen Cagle, Rte. 1, Twin Oaks Est, Claremore 74017

Sandy Cales, Rte. 1, Box 202A, Copan 74022

Nita Campbell, 9424 E. 40th Pl., Tulsa 74145

Mary Anne Cosper, 2915 S. 95th E. Ave., Tulsa 74129

Rose Cotner, Rte. 1, Bounds 74047

Carolyn Cox, Rte. 1, Box 252B, Duncan 73533

Jean Crider, Box 252, Perry 73077

Peggy Crow, 4936 S. 24th Place W., Tulsa 74107

Pat Crume, 621 N. Cherokee, Claremore 74017

Anna R. Dettweiler, Rte. 2, Box 214B, Watonga 73772

Gary Devine, Rte. 7, Box 181, Shawnee 74801

Doris Dodson, 3230 S. Florence, Tulsa 74105

Leah M. Dunn, 820 S. Sixth, Kingfisher 73950

Barbara Ellis, 5701 S. Rockford Pl., Tulsa 74105

Phyllis Evans, Rte. 7, Box 179B, Claremore 74017

Carolyn Fedde, 4704 S. 70th E. Ave., Tulsa 74145

Georgea Funk, P.O. Box 85, Woodward 73802

Shirley Gibbons, 440 Valley View Lane, Edmond 73034

Carole Gilliland, 4913 Bahama Ave., Sand Springs 74063

Maxine G. Ginn, Rte. 1, Box 60, Idabel 74745

Delores Gonser, Rte. 1, Box 723, Sharon 73856

Nadine Gotcher, 6634 E. 60th Pl., Tulsa 74145

Ellen L. Hill, Rte. 5, Box 49, Guthrie 73044

Helen Hill, 720 N. Oklahoma St., Guymon 73942

Darlene Hughes, 301 W. Sixth, Bristow 74010

Donna Johnson, 12725 E. 137th St. South, Broken Arrow 74012

Effie Johnson, 1326 E. Lincoln, Sapulpa 74066

Wanda Johnston, 1010 S. 6th, Ponca City 74601

Melody Keane, 1509 South Myssa Ave., Broken Arrow 74012

Donna Keasling, 6420 S.E. Baylor Dr., Bartlesville 74003

Betty Keith, 4719 S. Columbia Pl., Tulsa 74105

Judy Kimball, 12920 E. 101st N., Owasso 74055

Beula King, P.O. Box 370, Hugo 74743

Barbara Lancaster, 824 Delaware, Perry 73077

Dorothy Liniha, 1112 S.E. 17th, Pryor 74361

Della Littleton, Box 186, Custer 73639

Phyllis Lynn, 94205 187 E. Ave., Broken Arrow 74012

Betty Mansur, 5417 S. 76th E. Ave., Tulsa 74145

Vera McCoy, Rte. 5, Box 7, McAlester 74501

Wendy McCoy, Rte. 1, Box 99, Wilburton 74578

Mary McDermitt, 118 A. St., N.W., Ardmore 73401

Sandra McNaughton, Box 130, Collinsville 74021

Naomi Meeks, 2676 S. Richmond, Tulsa 74105
Iva Del Miller, Rte. 1, Box 144, Altus 73521
Nell Miller, P.O. Box 366, Boswell 74727
Rita Ann Mitchell, 305 S. Sixth, Broken Arrow 74012
Irene Moody, 16933 E. 21st St., Tulsa 74134
Betty Morgan, 200 S. 15th, Frederick 73542
Hazel Moseley, 3110 Maple Dr., Sand Springs 74063
Sondra Mullins, 7030 E. 77th, Tulsa 74133
Kathy Oldham, 1318 W. Cherokee, Enid 73701
Barbara Orton, 2338 W. Tecumseh, Tulsa 74127
Eileen Park, Rte. 1, Box 120, Ryan 73565
Gerri Parsons, 4030 Oklahoma Ave., Woodward 73801
Mildred Patterson, 501 E. Oklahoma, Guthrie 73044
Jennie Pease, P.O. Box 158, Alderson 74522
Margie A. Peterson, Rte. 7, Box 226, Claremore 74017
Carrol Piel, 601 Delaware St., Perry 73077
Tina Lee Plummer, 1300 Oxford Way, Rte. 3, Anadarko 73005
Collen Pollock, 603 N. 10th, Duncan 73533
Rosetta Preston, 7502 S. 70th Ave., Tulsa 74133
Brenda Punches, 10001 Allen Dr., Oklahoma City 73139
Edith Ramsey, 412 N. Sawyer, Pryor 74361
Margaret Reinaas, 4020 Westbrook, Stillwater 74074
Faye Rikkola, 804 N. Elm St., Owasso 74055
Carol Robertson, 924 Sparr, Seminole 74868
Jaquie M. Robertson, 8935 E. 49th St., Tulsa 74145
Shirley Rosamund, Rte. 2, Box 470, Broken Arrow 74012
Faith Irene Rowland, 11932 E. 37th Pl., Tulsa 74146
Linda Rudisill, 5218 E. 5th St., Tulsa 74112
Sue Sensintaffar, 705 W. Canton Ave., Broken Arrow 74012
Lis Ann Smith, 8944 E. 57th St., Tulsa 74145
Jewell Snyder, Rte. 3, Box 159DD, Altus 73521
Sue Spiva, 117 W. Seventh, Stillwater 74074
Gwynette Sturgess, Rte. 1, Box 34, Strang 74367
Martha Taylor, 1105 N.W. 16th, Lawton 73501
Lillard Xenia, 708 W. Sandy Rd., Atoka 74525
Cathy & Norman Yoss, 1101 N. Strong, McAlester 74501
Helen Young, Box 6, Manchester 73758

Oregon

Judy Bell, 250 S.E. Ventura Pl., Bend 97702
Elaine Killebrew, Box 626, Ontario 97914
Trudy Lynn Locks, P.O. Box 803, Roseburg 97470
Donna Santos, 14409 S.E. Alton Ct., Portland 97230

Dorothy Stout, 970 Airport Rd., Lebanan 97355
Mildred Stuwe, 1105 Savage Rd. N.E., Salem 97301

Pennsylvania

Nancy Alexander, 7220 Devonshire Heights, Harrisburg 17111
Betty Badgley, 38 Bittersweet Dr., Glen Mills 19243
Julie Bazewicz, 1212 E. 6th St., Berwick 18603
Nancy Blystone, R.D. 1, Allen Rd., Cambridge Springs 16403
Gloria Brosious, 199 Window Ave., Southampton 18966
Charmaine Cesar, 714 Mt. Ave., Pen Argyl 18072
Jean Deitrick, P.O. Box B, Benton 17814
Patricia Diettrich, 100 Roosevelt Ave., McKee Rocks 15136
Ruth Anne Edwards, Box 302 Main St., Schaefferstown 17088
Dorothy Falcone, 508 English Rd., Bath 18014
Bee Figuly, 2540 Blossom Lane, New Castle 16105
Billie Fleming, 384 New Castle Rd., Butler 16001
Pepper Aubrey George, 2915 Whitewood Rd., Bethlehem 18016
Bernie Hieber, c/o 2079 E. Tioga St., Philadelphia 19134
Shirley A. Humes, R.D. 3, Box 117, Meadville 16335
Gloria Jones, 112 Stump Rd., R.D. 1, North Wales 19454
Rella L. Keller, 790 Joy Dr., Greencastle 17225
Geri King, 1798 Davison Rd., Harborcreek 16421
Joan Koser, 37 Cedar Manor Rd. 14, Elizabeth 17022
Elinor Meyer, P.O. Box 703, Doylestown 18901
Carol Myer, 1000 W. Ingomar Rd., Pittsburgh 15237
Edith Nelson, 312 Belmont Ave., Mt. Pocono 18344
Carol Peters, 3665 Backus Rd., Harborcreek 16421
Kay Probst, R.D. 1, Stillwater 17878
Jo Ann Schlosser, 137 Ensminger, Jacobus 17407
Ruth Schrader, 539 Reagan St., Sunbury 17801
Janice D. Sherman, 3595 Brownsville Rd., Pittsburgh 15227
Gail Snaman, 855 Bridgewater Dr., Pittsburgh 15216
Glendora B. Vanorder, 100 Shady Lane, Carlisle 17013
Betty Lou Witmer, 211 Hilltop Rd., Boiling Springs 17007
Diane Zufall, Rte. 2, Box 275, Mt. Pleasant 15666

Rhode Island

Nancy Landry, 26 Firelade Ave., Riverside 02915
Cheryl Merolla, 567 Putnam Pike, Greenville 02828
Jeanne Serpa, P.O. Box 1259, Glenwood Dr., Charlestown 02813
Laurie M. Smith, Box 31, Kenyon 02836

South Carolina

Betty Agnew, 612 Lyman St., Gaffney 29340

Peggy Anderson, 1203 Collins Park St., Conway 29526

Cherie Brannan, 120 Briarwood Ln., Summerville 29483

Juanita Brovillette, 146 Bailey Ave., Rock Hill 29730

Wayne N. Carter, 1579 Edisto Dr., Orangeburg 29115

Lib Coleman, Rte. 3, Box 58-A, Travelers Rest 29690

Launa Cramer, 10 Woodmont Circle, Greenville 29605

John E. Howison, 299 Plantation Rd., Rock Hill 29730

Margaret D. Howison, 299 Plantation Rd., Rock Hill 29730

Mildred Knight, 405 Woodland Dr., Lancaster 29720

Beatrice Ladd, 9B Stillwell Manor, Inman 29349

Judith Lawing, 605 Jasmine Ave., Myrtle Beach 29577

Dianna Satterfield, Rte. 3, P.O. Box 118, Moore 29369

Jo Schwartz, 208 Devon Dr., Mauldin 19662

Val Steele, 142 Green Bay Dr., Rock Hill 29730

A. Jean White, Rte. 2, 601 Belle Ile Rd., Georgetown 29440

Charlene Youngblood, P.O. Box 2794, Myrtle Beach 29577

Tennessee

Edith Beaty, 400 Green Acres, Memphis 38117

Lou Breeding, 202 S. First, Union City 38261

Martha Brewer, 2751 Stage Park Dr., Memphis 38134

Georgia Buckner, 1719 Old Lascossas Rd., Murfreesboro 37130

Nancy Bowie Carter, 915 Anderson St., Bristol 37620

Mary Collins, Rte. 2, Box 408, Camden 38320

Barbara Decker, Northgate Mall, Tallahoma 37388

Jane Dryden, 2033 North Locust, P.O. Box 336, Lawrenceburg 38464

Dana Easton, 3972 Jackson Ave., Memphis 38128

Margaret Grace, 4752 Linda Lane, Memphis 38117

Ann Gray, 3933 Wisteria, Memphis 38116

Frieda Hamm, 144 Cypress Ave., Selmer 39375

Cathy Johnson, 4036 Beechdale Cove, Memphis 38128

Cornelia M. Judd, 5001 Bell Rd. Q1, Hermitage 37076

Betty Maier, 3930 Patte Ann Dr., Memphis 38116

Joyce Longworth McBee, 314 Old New Era Rd., Sevierville 37862

Patty McKnight, 7666 Hwy. 51N, Millington 38053

Charlotte Pickens, 1511 Country Club Ct., Franklin 37064

Rebecca Ponte, P.O. Box 17129, Nashville 37217

Suzy Ramsey, 4525 Old Stage Rd., Kingsport 37614

Gayle Roberts, Rte. 11, Box 350E, Crossville 38555

Margaret Rosenbloom, 63 Summar Dr., Jackson 38301

Rieta Selberg, 2020 Whispering Pines, Germantown 38138

Jean Y. Sloan, 5005 Collinwood Dr., Clarksville 37042

Joan Stamper, 123 Franklin, P.O. Box 415, Clarksville 38053

Marjory Stumpenhorst, Rte. 1, Sharon Lane, Jackson 38301

Wayne Suite, 103 Postwood Pl., Nashville 37205

Karen M. Tate, 1520 Central Ave., Memphis 38104

Loias P. Vaughan, 1414B Poplar M.1, Murfreesboro 37130

Evelyn Welty, Rte. 7, Box 252, Lebanon 37087

Ann Williams, 1900 Randolph Pl., Nashville 37202

Audrey Wright, Rte. 1, Box 272, Murfreesboro 37130

Dot York, P.O. Box 1765, 816 Lakeside Dr., Fairfield Glade 38555

Texas

Elaine Adamek, Rte. 5, Box 261X, Victoria 77901

Anita Annucci, 19963 Encino Royale, San Antonio 78232

Nancy Atkinson, 108 Saint Jo Terr., Nacona 76255

Noreen Banes, 2107 Albert Rd., Carrolton 75007

Sarah Bateman, 4831 Casemont, Spring 77373

J. Ann Bauerkemper, 613 Sky Forest, San Antonio 78232

Juanita Belcher, 1511 Ave. C, Denton 76201

Noram J. Belcher, Rte. 2, Box 242E, Sequin 78155

Margie Boylan, Rte. 2, Box 137, Wichita Falls 76367

Marilyn Bradley, 2032 Houston Pl., Denton 76201

Rosa Brashier, Rte. 1, Box 254, Hillsboro 76645

Pat Brass, 5010 Spencer, Pasadena 77501

Miriam Brooks, 8342 San Fernando Way, Dallas 75218

Kathryn Buckley, 101 Oakhurst Dr., Palestine 75801

Grace Bulla, 907 Charles, Panhandle 79068

Peggy Caldwell, 62 Meyer Rd., Huffman 77336

Ann Carlton, Rte. 1, Box 439, Denton 76201

Helen Carpenter, 1605 Marquette Dr., Richardson 75081

Novella Carson, 204 S. Race, Lampasas 76550

Jean Chancelor, 5611 Briargrove, Wichita Falls 76310

Edwina Cline, 2627 Albans, Houston 77005

Melida Coleman, 1010 Laredo St., Laredo 78040

Beckye Conklin, Rte. 2, Muleshoe 79347

Alice Frances Vickery Conner, 4633 Rose of Sharon Lane, Fort Worth 76137

Maliza W. Cox, 3112 Drexel Dr., Dallas 75205

Susette Davenport, P.O. Box 415, Brenham 77833

Faith Delevante, 2006 Fair Meadow Dr., Arlington 76012

Nettie Lee Dinn, 335 Oak Glen, San Antonio 78206

Jackie Dodge, 27170 Afton Way, Huffman 77336

Mary Domec, P.O. Box 188, Jasper 75951

Sharon Drewfs & Col. H.F. Drewfs, Jr., 77006 Rusk Circle, Fort Hood 76544

Cindy Dunagan, 2009 W. Eighth, Fort Stockton 79735

Selena Earle, 302 Milton, Jacksonville 75766

Johnnye Echols, 8647 Capri, Dallas 75238

June Ehlers, 5008 Green Oaks Dr., Plano 75023

Vicky Eidson, 515 Exeter Rd., Apt. K2, San Antonio 78209

Jerry E. Engler, R.D. 2, Box 133, Bowie 76230

Barbara Epperson, 4107 Birdwell Dr., Tyler 75701

Jimi Ewing, 107 N. Main, Miami 75354

Loraine Fears, 208 Richmond, Angleton 77515

Anna Fox, 742 Rosewood, Boerne 78006

Betty Gann, Professional Bldg., Daggett St., Pecos 79772

Shirley M. Gaultney, 806 Finale, San Antonio 78216

Carol Gerk, Rte. 4, Box 42, Herford 79045

Barbara Gibson, Box 983, Kilgore 75662

Ruth Gooch, 812 E. 4th, Denver City 79323

Edith Green, 1208 Tarnerick Dr., Mexia 76667

Mary Haddigan, 1401 Cavalier #654, Richardson 75080

Ruth Hancock, 100 W. Walnut, Decatur 76234

Viola Hardgrave, Rte. 5, Box 301, Palestine 75801

Milly Haring, 315 N. Travis, Sherman 75090

Pat Harmon, 3605 Bluff St., Wichita Falls 76302

Samie Harrison, P.O. Box 226, Petrolia 76377

Connie Harvis, 6261 Goliad, Apt. A, Dallas 75214

Ruth Heasley, Box 683, Fulton 78358

Ann Heck, 111 Woodbine Dr., Palestine 75801

Rudy Henderson, 1203 Baylor Dr., Longview 75601

Mary Henry, P.O. Box 1693, Plainview 79072

Virginia Hernlund, 10102 Osprey Ct., Austin 78750

Carolyn Hewitt, 507 N. Bradley, McKinney 75069

Mary Ellen Hillis, 201 W. Niblick, Longview 75604

Winnie Hinger, 3833 Ridgeoak, Dallas 75234

Betty Holladay, 1201 Adams St., Conroe 77301

Helen Holland, 702 Pecan, Bonham 75418

Vivian Houghtling, 225 Main, Eagle Pass 78852

Mary Houlette, 910 N.E. 4th, Dumas 79029

Betty J. Jaynes, 2300 N. Shore Dr., Bonham 75418

Jean Jennings, 3024 N. Vernon, Amarillo 79107

Marilynn Z. Johnson, 1302 State Line, Texarkana 75502

Beth Johnston, Box 217B, Rte. 2, Palestine 75801

Barbara Jones, 1115 Central Blvd., Brownsville 78520

June Jones, Rte. 4, Box 105D, Rockwall 75087

Miki Jones, 3500 Sublett Rd., Arlington 76017

Nine Judd, 419 N. Maple, Stratford 77477

Annie May Jurcak, 909 W. 12th St., Plainview 79072

Florence E. Kolaitis, 174 Southwood Dr., Lancaster 75146

Delores Leach, 5926 Broadway, Galveston 77551

Leona Leland, 1701 Kansas Ave., San Angelo 76904

Mary Lewis, 2279 Triway Lane, Houston 77701

Jeanette Lukeman, 803 Attow, Brenham 77833

Mary McKibben, Rte. 10, Box 2364, Odessa 79763

Kathi McKinzie, 305 Zephyr, Plainview 79072

Martha McLean, 3302 Pleasant Grove Rd., Texarkana 75501

Ruth Medaris, 2312 South, Kilgore 75662

Charlotte Miller, 1306 Sandy Circle, Irving 75060

Kaye Miller, 6715 Cypress Point Dr., Houston 77069

Theresa Milton, 19963 Encino Royale, San Antonio 78232

Irene Moore, 112 Meadbrook, Palestine 75801

Margaret Morgan, 620 Donna Lane, Bedford 76021

Norabeth Morton, Rte. 5, Box 226F, Palestine 75801

Jamie Murray, 603 Locust St., Angleton 77515

Phillis Neff, 8206 Colonial Oaks, Spring 77379

Eva Nixon, 2654 34th, Lubbock 79408

Ida Lee Parkman, 107 Bellview Dr., Palestine 75801

Betty Partridge, 1702 Lexington, Deer Park 77536

Rose Ann Pool, 3419 Pearl St., Nacogdoches 75961

Mona Post, 15907 Echo Hill Dr., Clear Lake City 77059

Mary Gayle Reagan, P.O. Box 562, Daingerfield 75638

Eunice Rubel, 540 Ferry Dr., Bridge City 77611

Doris Rudd, Gail Rte., Gail 79738

Margaret Silar, 303 S. Ross, Mexia 76667

Audrey Smith, 4242 S. Fifth, Abilene 79065

Ruth Smith, Rte. 3, Box 138AB, Jacksonville 75766

Angie Stephen, Rte. 2, Box 209, Weatherford 76086

Mary Stewart, S. Plain Mall B13, Lubbock 79414

Jan Sursa, Rte. 2, Box 2154, San Antonio 78006

Alva Lee Theilg, 5430 Chenna, Houston 77096

Audrey Tweed, 324 White Rock, N. Shopping Center, Dallas 75238

Jean Uerling, 3904 Golden Oaks, Fort Worth 76117

Flo Viles, 4801 Roberts Dr., Lewisville 75056

Betty Walker, 11526 Wolf Run, Houston 77701

Joanne J. Webb, 5318 Hemlock, Baytown 77521

Barbara West, 3713 Dartmouth, Garland 75043

Betty Westcott, P.O. Box 1047, Livingston 77351

Pat Wheeler, 108 N. Crescent, Electra 76360

Joey Williams, 3437 Flamingo Way, Mesquite 75150

Adaline Wittie, 1240 Rice Rd., San Antonio 78220

Kathy Woehl, 916 Deorsam Dr., Copperas Cove 76522

Utah

Wilda J. Diehl, 13 Sumac Way, Brigham City 84301

Betty Headman, 1082 590 E., Orem 84057

Sharon Peterson, 58 W. Gentile, Layton 84041

Dorothy F. Williams, 44 Oak Lane, Kaysville 84037

Eleanor Zimmerman, P.O. Box 7620, Salt Lake City 84110

Kim Zimmerman, 4370 S. 300 W., Salt Lake City 84110

Vermont

Muriel A. Bohne, Harwood Hill, Bennington 05201
Ellie Martin, A & P Shopping Center, Essex Junction 05452

Virginia

Patti Bondi, 2155 Veenendaa Ct., Herndon 22070
Penny Carroll, 4412 Ben Franklin, Virginia Beach 23462
Mary Margaret De Hart, 153 Benedict Ave., Langley AFB 23665
Diane Theresa Dodd, 12156 Holly Knoll Circle, Great Falls 22066
Emma Duncan, 7439 Major Ave., Norfolk 23505
Susan A. Elmore, P.O. Box 1535, Petersburg 23805
Sheila Ferree, 909 Indian Ridge Rd., Lynchburg 21502
June B. Garrison, 2605 River Oaks Dr., Chesapeake 23321
Janet Goldbach, 2123 Hollybriar Pt., Norfolk 23518
Jackie Heupel, 6409 Wyngate Dr., Springfield 22152
Anne Higgins, 2038 Plank Rd., Fredericksburg 22401
Mary Jo Jennings, Box 3070, Martinsville 24112
Shirley Jones, 7599 Woodstown Dr., Springfield 22153
Rena Kramer, 121 Twin Creek Terr., Forest 24551
Diane Lane, 598 Minuteman Dr., Newport News 23602
Betty J. Leary, Rte. 3, Box 180A, Amherst 24521
Carolyn Lucas, 230 A. Gray Ave., Langley AFB 23665
Jane B. Ludwig, CDT, P.O. Box 412, White Stone 22578
Janet Ryburn, 104 Franklin St., Bluefield 24605
Rosemarie Schwindt, 2408 Heutte Dr., Norfolk 23501
Roslyn Stallcup, 1436 Lakeview Dr., Virginia Beach 23462
Carol Staton, Rte. 3, Box 645 A, Ashland 23005
Elizabeth Tush, 1608 Chatham Rd., Waynesboro 22980

Washington

Hazel Behar, 707 Hillside Dr., Yakima 98903
Linda Bourland, 3816 E. Evergreen Blvd., Vancouver 98661
Shirley Charette, 7713 47th W., Tacoma 98466
Margaret J. Dillard, 1220 Mount Whitney Dr., Vancouver 98664
Elizabeth Duvall, 65 Windship Dr., Kala Pl., Port Townsend 98368
Wallace Foulkes, 6106 99th St. S.W., Tacoma 98499
Rose Marie Pierce, 115 W. 11th, Port Angeles 98362
Allegra Sampson, 518 W. Entiat Ave., Kennewick 99336
Barbara Williams, 405 S. Buntin, Kennewick 99336
Barbara Youngers, Rte. 1, 705 E. N.W., Ephrata 98823

West Virginia

Irene R. Anderson, Homestead Dr., Williamstown 26187
Stephanie Ballard, 1812 Coffman St., Barboursville 25504
Joanne Britton, 210 Henry St., Ravenswood 26164
Gloria Crouch, P.O. Box 631, Summersville 26651
Melanie Dailey, 133 S. 2nd St., Paden City 26159
Shirley Greathouse, 1723 20th Ave., Parkersburg 26101
Virginia McClung, P.O. Box 164, Lewisburg 24901
Dorothy B. Neal, 3147 Saltwell Rd., Huntington 25701
John Peg, 338 Cottage Ave., Weston 26452
Sue Persinger, 121 Watson Ave., Shrewsburg 25184
Juanita Redmond, Box 324, Boomer 25031
Virginia Sue Sharps, R.D. 4, Bellovedere, Wheeling 26003

Wisconsin

Rose M. Ault, 340 N. Military Ave., Green Bay 54303
Kathy Bilstrom, 4759 N. Larkin, Whitefish Bay 53211
Barb Bosler, 6751 Otter Lane, Lake Tomahawk 54539
Elizabeth Brudos, 307 Kertzman Pl., Lacrosse 54601
Shirley Calhoun, P.O. Box 96, Aniwa 54408
Mary Ann Chucka, 4464 N. 77th St., Milwaukee 53218
Kathy Geis, R.R. 4, Fond du Lac 54935
Norma Harrinton, 11011 N. Granville Rd., Mequon 53092
Molly Hoople, 290 Doty St., Fond du Lac 54935
Mona Kochendorfer, Rte. 1, Box 312, Colfax 54730
Eleanor Little, Box 209, Main St., Lavalle 53941
Karen Maron, Rte. 2, Columbus 53925
Dorothy Polyak, Rte. 2, Box 1469A, Wild Rose 54984
Rose Rosenberg, 810 E. Grant, Eau Claire 54701
Martha Jane Schult, Rte. 2, La Crosse 54601
Bob Smith, 7940 W. Layton Ave., Milwaukee 53220
Irene Spoerl, 841 Atwood Ave., Park Falls 54552
Mary Stryker, 2539 9th St., Monroe 53566

Wyoming

Marietta Armstrong, 1823 E. 17th St., Cheyenne 82001
Eleanor Hewgley, 1116 Cactus Hill Rd., Cheyenne 82001
Claudie Meyer, Box 236, Pinedale 82941
Delchia, Neighbors, Box 230, Sheridan 82801
Barbara Ullrich, 768 Ranger, Cheyenne 82001

Africa

Mary McLean, P.O. Box 41754, Nairobi, Kenya

England and Canada

Barbara Bassett, 615 Lansdowne, Westmount H3Y 2V7, Canada

Martine Cheval, 20 Mississauga Valley Blvd., Mississauga, Ontario L5A 3S1, Canada

Helen Cocksutt, 59-50 Fidlers Green Rd., London, Ontario N6H 4T4, Canada

Brenda Conroy, 6 Water St., St. Marys, Ontario, Canada

Kathleen Dunn, 4 McRarle Ave., Atikokan, Ontario P0T 1C0, Canada

Elizabeth Earle, South Pill Cottage, South Pill Saltash, Cornwall, England

Barbara Edney, R.R. 1, Churchill, Ontario L0L 1K0, Canada

Delma Green, 5 Pine St., Dartmouth, Nova Scotia B2Y 3Z3, Canada

Sheila Heck, Box 216, Coaldale, Alberta, Canada

Maya Johnson, R.R. 3, Kings County, Centerville N.S. B0P 1J0, Canada

Helen J. Marchyn, 127 Lockhart Dr., Saint Catharines, Ontario L2T 1W3, Canada

Audrey Neale, 70 Baif Blvd., Apt. 803, Toronto, Ontario L4C 5L2, Canada

Shirley J. Patterson, 1302 Grafton Ave., Moose Jaw, Saskatchewan S6H 8S8, Canada

Gail Perks, 17 O'Hara Dr., Halifax, Nova Scotia B3M 2E8, Canada

Kate Roed, 424 Beverly St., Winnipeg, Manitoba R3G 1T8, Canada

Brigitte Roseman, 35 Cedarland Dr., Brantford, Ontario N3R 6G8, Canada

Linda J. Seely, Box 333 Stirling, Alberta T0K 2E0, Canada

Valerie Skemp, 593 Egret Ct., Richmond, B.C. V7F 3W2, Canada

Ruth Smith, R.R. 1, Wilmont, Nova Scotia B0P 1N0, Canada

Bernice Wishart, 264 Varsity Crescent N.W., Alberta T3B 226, Canada

Kathy Woolsel, 2842 Heath Dr., Victoria, B.C. V9A 2J5, Canada

Index

Page numbers in italics refer to illustrations and patterns. The color insert follows page 38.

About the Author

She starts each seminar with "HELLO EVERYBODY" and a laugh that is loud, spontaneous, and contagious. Priscilla Hauser insists she can teach anyone to paint, and she has proved it. In the past 25 years she has published more than 50 books on the various forms of painting, taught up to 350 students a week at her Little Red Tole House, and inspired countless TV viewers in her successful PBS series *The Magic of Decorative Painting*.

At the tender age of 12, Priscilla was introduced to her first decorative painting. A friend had received a hand-painted bedroom furniture set for Christmas which absolutely fascinated Priscilla. She went to the woman who had painted the furniture and asked if she could take lessons. The woman told Priscilla she was not a teacher, but in the course of the conversation, she referred to the trunk as being "tole-painted."

In 1959 Priscilla took a six-week course at the YWCA in Kansas City on "tole painting." After that she painted absolutely everything she could get her hands on and she hasn't stopped.

In 1961 Priscilla and her husband moved to Tulsa and bought their first home. In response to neighbors who asked if she would teach them how to tole paint, Priscilla Hauser developed her unique methods of teaching.

Priscilla taught classes in her garage until neighbors complained about too much "traffic" in the neighborhood. At that time she moved her studio to the back of a paint store and the following year opened the renowned Priscilla's Little Red Tole House. In 1966 she founded the National Tole and Decorative Painting Seminars. Today there are more than 3,000 Priscilla Hauser accredited teachers around the world. These are people who have studied with her for 100 hours or more at one of her National Seminars. These people are listed beginning on page 95.

In 1972 Priscilla founded the National Society of Tole and Decorative Painters. She served as its first president and housed its national office at the Little Red Tole House for the first year and a half. Today the Society has more than 25,000 members and chapters throughout the world.

Priscilla loves to teach in her beautiful little Victorian "studio by the sea," which she opened in July 1985. It is located on the Gulf of Mexico where the sand is snow white and the aquamarine water sparkles like diamonds. She also teaches in Tulsa and on occasion travels throughout the country teaching. For a Seminar brochure and information on classes and seminars, write to: Priscilla's Little Red Tole House, Inc., P.O. Box 521013, Tulsa, OK 74152.

For information on how you can have **Better Homes and Gardens** delivered to your door, write to Mr. Robert Austin, P.O. Box 4536, Des Moines, IA 50336.